CHANNEL
KINDNESS

CHANNEL KINDNESS

Stories of Kindness and Community

**BORN THIS WAY FOUNDATION REPORTERS
WITH LADY GAGA**

FEIWEL AND FRIENDS
NEW YORK

CONTENT WARNING

The material in this book covers topics that include sexual assault, suicidal ideation, and other potentially triggering subjects.

A FEIWEL AND FRIENDS BOOK

An imprint of Macmillan Publishing Group, LLC

120 Broadway, New York, NY 10271

CHANNEL KINDNESS: STORIES OF KINDNESS AND COMMUNITY. Copyright © 2020 by Born This Way Foundation.
All rights reserved.
Printed in China by RR Donnelley Asia Printing Solutions Ltd., Dongguan City, Guangdong Province.

Our books may be purchased in bulk for promotional, educational, or business use. Please contact your local bookseller or the Macmillan Corporate and Premium Sales Department at (800) 221-7945 ext. 5442 or by email at MacmillanSpecialMarkets@macmillan.com.

Library of Congress Cataloging-in-Publication Data is available.

ISBN 978-1-250-24558-8 (hardcover) / ISBN 978-1-250-24557-1 (ebook)

Book design by Mallory Grigg and Trisha Previte

Feiwel and Friends logo designed by Filomena Tuosto

First edition, 2020

10 9 8 7 6 5 4 3 2 1

fiercereads.com

We dedicate this book to any and all humans who inevitably suffer in life. For those who both do and do not yet understand the power of channeling kindness into all the things we do. And to kindness itself. You're the best. Thank you.

Love, your kindness punks

Lady Gaga

Cynthia Germanotta   *M Oates*

TABLE OF OF CONT

ENTS

BEGINNING

As I scanned the pages of this incredible compilation of kindness, bravery, community, resilience, and triumph, I was overwhelmed with pride, gratitude, and appreciation for the people sharing their stories with me, with you, and with the world. Contained in these pages is the proof of a kinder, braver world that I envisioned more than eight years ago when I cofounded Born This Way Foundation with my mother, the proof that I had so desperately prayed for as a young girl, and the proof that I've tried to work tirelessly for over my lifetime.

Though I was surrounded by love, I often lived in the world by myself—whether writing and performing songs on the piano, creating elaborate stories and performances in the most unlikely of situations, turning strangers into friends at restaurants where I waitressed, or, unfortunately, trying to escape the harsh reality of bullies and the unkindness that often surrounded me. The world that I created in my dreams was one in which people led with kindness, were emboldened by bravery, and accumulated love and community. As I read the stories contained within these pages—stories of standing up for love, standing up for others, and the quiet courage it takes to stand up for yourself—I believed the world I created in my dreams could one day be possible for everyone else, too.

Our book, told from the vantage point of young people from all across the country, highlights random acts of kindness given to and by strangers during periods of grief, loneliness, and hardship. It emphasizes the connection and tender care that come with building genuine friendships. And it is a gentle reminder of the kindness and love we all have the potential to share. I can see that through the hearts and passion of the young people in our Born This Way Foundation family, our kinder, braver world is becoming a reality.

Born This Way Foundation was a movement before it was formalized as an organization. The same can be said of Channel Kindness, which I refer to as the kindest place on the internet and now—the kindest place in print. Both were built out of the experiences that I had growing up and the profound impact that kindness (and its absence) has had on my life. As I began to tour the world, I would share my experiences onstage, and thousands of young people from all over the world would share theirs with me. We would cry together, laugh together, heal together, and promise one another that we'd continue to not only survive, but that we would find a way to thrive.

It was in that spirit—and with *their* spirit—that we started our work at Born This Way Foundation for a generation of young people who shouldn't have to live in a brave, kind world that only exists in their heads. Our goals at the foundation (and I would venture, in our lives—for the team of people who have made this work their mission) are threefold: to make kindness cool; to validate the emotions of young people around the world; and to eliminate the stigma surrounding mental health. It will take *all* of us to accomplish these lofty goals, and we believe that young people are uniquely positioned to create this kinder, braver world because they are filled with hope, compassion, and a commitment to community, and they are defined by diversity, inclusivity, and a distinct perseverance that make them powerful beyond even their own wildest imaginations. In each interaction I have with young people, I see this. And you will see this here, too, on every page, in every story.

Lady Gaga

THE VALUE OF NEGATIVE SPACE

LADY GAGA

When I was young, I prayed a lot. (Whether that implicitly means that someone should or should not read this book, however, is decidedly irrelevant.) It wasn't because I was religious. It was because I was a deep and passionate thinker—who thought a lot—and was spiritual and creative even when I was very little. So if we substitute *prayer* with *asking the universe questions about my life*, this, to me, would be a more accurate way for you to understand the beginning of my story as Lady Gaga and why it is important to read and share this book with others. I always considered myself a theorist and would posture ideas constantly to myself and those around me. *Who am I? What am I? Who are we as humankind?* Then I began channeling this into inventions: music, characters in school plays, poetry, and writing. Needless to say, at some point, lots of people have found me to be very peculiar. *Weird* was a word I heard a lot. *Why do you want to be a singer, actress, dancer, performer, artist, writer?* was also condescendingly asked of me. And to be honest, it ultimately felt as though many relentless and quite mean children and adults around me were asking me why I existed. Because I never felt I existed without art.

Middle school acting headshot

Thus began my journey with bullying. I was even bullied in class for essays similar to the one you're reading right now. Once I gave a dissertation my senior year of high school. I practiced it all night; it was about shock art and representations of Christianity in art throughout history, the latter being the point of my homework and the former being the conceptual twist I threw in to make all eighty pages of my thesis interesting to me. I distinctly recall a moment—one of many stories that made me who I am. I was delivering my thesis as a speech to my class, with poster boards I'd beautifully made to show the evolution of God in art from classical to contemporary, and my teacher was called out of the room for an emergency and asked me to continue my presentation. In the middle of my speech, my high school bully—in front of my entire class—loudly and rudely interrupted me and said, "Why are you still talking?" Now, because this is a book and not a movie or episodic show on Netflix, I can't do an impression of her to truly do her justice, but let's just say her tone was the equivalent of *You're annoying and dumb* and *Could you please spare me and this entire class of your idiotic attempt to care about this assignment.*

I was upset that I actually did something I hadn't done so openly before. I used to cry at home or in the school bathroom or the nurse's office, but this time, I burst into tears in front of my entire class and sobbed uncontrollably with my hands over my face while everyone stared at me. When my teacher reentered the room, I very quickly composed myself and continued to share my project. The only thing worse for me in this moment than having a breakdown in public in front of my bully would have been my teacher catching on, asking me who bullied me, and then me having to lie or tell the truth—both of which would have gotten me in trouble, either in school or socially with the other students.

So that was that. And even as I type this, it reminds me of how flippantly my tribulations as a young person both came and went without anything to remedy them. They were over as quickly as that last sentence. Once I was thrown in a trash can on a street corner by a group of boys that were friends with my bully. (They were instructed to do so.) I distinctly recall the laughter and joy they took in humiliating me while shouting, "That's where you belong!" When I was younger, I was also pinched in the hallway by older girls who would grip my arm tightly and whisper to me, "You're a slut," as I walked to class. They were jealous that the older boys at our brother school paid a lot of attention to me. Funnily enough, this impacted me so much that I even feel the need to clarify while writing this for you—I was most certainly not a slut.

I'm leaving out a lot because there's so much to say, I would have to write an entire book myself. Having depression, anorexia, bulimia, anxiety, and masochistic tendencies that included scratching or cutting my arms with knives when I was in emotional distress. This went on from age eleven till rather recently in my early thirties, and I still struggle with some of these things.

I imagine my brain is like a pinball machine with uncomfortable marbles, and each one of my obstacles is a marble. Every once in a while, one or a few shoot out and I can either gain points for dealing with them using skills I've learned, suffer while they fall past the flippers into an abyss of panic, or just hope they roll back into the trigger slot and keep quiet so I don't have to play pinball wizard with my mental issues. What I really wish to make a point of is: amidst all this, eventually I became a famous artist, but all of these things came with me.

Becoming a star does not fix anything. In fact, the demands of it made it all the more complicated. Imagine having an eating disorder and just after a segment on prime time news about the current state of the US's attack on terrorism, there is a report that you have gained weight, with a photo of you onstage where you clearly have gained weight and a news anchor actually discussing and gawking at how unattractive you now are.

Fantastic. Cut to me in a hotel room somewhere on a world tour having a panic attack over a fear of my body image that I've had for so long I don't know who I am without it.

I went on to achieve things beyond my wildest imagination, and I was still haunted and plagued by massive insecurities and mental health problems that emerged—PTSD being one of them. I've tried to understand my pain, solve it like a detective. I've driven myself crazy trying to even understand that once I became an adult, I was still not equipped to handle all I had been through, and that it made me even more prone to being controlled and bullied in my business. At least it didn't control my art. I'm brave in some places, less brave in others. My trauma history is extensive; I've spoken about it at length, and in a semi-healed as well as semi-detached way, I can once again admit that I was repeatedly raped when I was nineteen by someone in the music industry and as I got sicker and sicker mentally on tour after my career took off, no one helped me until I essentially went rogue. I became so self-aware of how sick I was becoming, I locked myself in my apartment in New York and told everyone to leave me alone while I painted. Basically, this was code for *Lady Gaga quits*.

I grew up around alcoholism and developed a neuropathic pain condition—which is essentially, when I get stressed, I feel physical pain throughout my entire body. It's so excruciating I can barely think. Yet here I am writing this to you. I think finally in my life, I have at least figured out the through line of all the things I've been through.

In every instance, there was an absence of kindness.

In most instances, it was only when someone shared their painful stories with me that I no longer felt invisible and became less afraid.

So then I developed a theory of The Value of Negative Space. The currency of understanding the gravity of what can happen when kindness is absent. There was a moment of silence after I cried in front of my class when my bully made fun of me, and I've learned now that those moments of quiet, when we don't always know what to do, should be filled with kindness. What I find to be interesting is, there are actually two negative spaces that possess value: one that is empty, quiet, and ignores the absence of kindness; and another that is filled with negativity. Filling this space is my life now. This is this book. This is what my bully taught me. Sure, being bullied versus being raped may sound like it has a clear winner if it were a kindness competition, but the truth is trauma is not a contest, and every story in this book is equally valuable.

It's important to pause and think about what you're doing, just in case you might hurt someone. And by someone, that includes yourself.

Don't just respond
with kindness:
fill the empty with it.

Together, we can bring positivity into negative space. ♥

- TRUST -

Kindness

CHARLEEN COLÓN

On a gloomy afternoon in December 2013, two days before Christmas, my family's doorbell rang. Not much in the mood for an unannounced visit from a friend—much less a stranger—I felt little enthusiasm as I went to see who it was.

Most years I look forward to the holiday season with childlike wonder. No matter what challenges might be going on, I'm usually so happy just smelling the fresh pine tree in the middle of our house and seeing it hung with ornaments, twinkling with lights as wrapped presents grow in numbers daily. Christmas for me has always been a time of family, food, and friends and of reliving happy memories of holidays past and making new ones.

Sadly, though, on the day when our doorbell rang unexpectedly, I felt unable to partake in the spirit of the season. At the time, I had recently experienced a deep and devastating loss: the death of my mother. Without her in my life, the world seemed suddenly to have become darker and colder. The idea that I was supposed to feel good again just because of the holiday was almost a cruel joke.

"Are you Charleen?" asked the kind-looking man standing on my doorstep. He was a man I had never met before, in his early forties and athletic in appearance, with bright eyes and a look of both confidence and compassion.

"Yes," I answered, warmed by his thoughtful smile—at least, warmed enough that I chose to trust him.

With that, he handed me a holiday card and nodded, encouraging me to open it in front of him.

My first thought was *Who hand-delivers a card in the middle of the holiday rush?* But rather than say anything, I went ahead and invited him inside and opened the card as he waited. It read:

Inside the envelope was a total of $500 in gift cards.

Like magic, it seemed, a stranger had made the effort to do something so kind, good, caring and, frankly, surprising that I wasn't sure whether to cry or laugh for joy. Somehow he must have known that it was always my mom who managed to find time and resources to shop for everything on my list. Had someone told him that without her, the season was going to be an especially lean one for our family? His generosity meant much more than being able to buy presents that year. His gift let me know that even though Mom was no longer alive, I could still connect to her love through thoughtful acts of kindness. They were there to remind me that the world didn't have to be such a dark and cold place after all.

The man wouldn't have stayed longer, but I explained that I had a few questions—starting with his name and where he was from. At forty-three years old, Christopher Chiarenza was a successful entrepreneur from Long Island.

As I soon learned, I was not the first—or the last—recipient of Christopher's generosity. Usually he prefers to remain anonymous, but he had made an exception in my case and then agreed that I could share his story, if only to encourage others to find a way, as he had, to pay it forward.

When Christopher was young, he too lost a parent—his father. The death of his first role model and number-one inspiration took a profound toll on him. He told me that, for some years, he felt deprived of one of the most positive influences in his life. His saving grace, he explained, was learning to look to his faith—especially in darker times. From the teachings of his religion and the examples of other role models in his spiritual community, Christopher embraced the core belief that you reap what you sow. He says it's not only a proven truth in his life but also a principle that he believes can apply to others as the law of the land.

Before he came to that realization, Christopher admitted, there was a time in his early twenties when he didn't fully appreciate the value of kindness.

"How so?" I asked.

He described the type of person he is today as different from the type of person he was twenty years ago. Back then, he said, "I was very self-absorbed." When he reached his thirties and started to seriously examine his priorities, Christopher chose to show his thanks to all who had helped him by carving out a new path toward helping others.

The moment he opened his eyes to the ways he could make a difference in his own community, he discovered how great the need really was.

The moment he opened his eyes to the ways he could make a difference in his own community, he discovered how great the need really was. Feeling that he had been blessed financially, he opted to perform acts of kindness in the form of monetary assistance. Over the years, Christopher has continued his practice of generosity, especially during the holidays.

As it was for me, the holiday season happens to be a time when many are often most in need, a time when they ought to be enjoying the happiness of the season but may be feeling low and alone. In order to select the beneficiaries of his good deeds, Christopher invites people from his community to suggest names and stories of those who could most use a kind gift of hope and help.

I had to ask him, "After sharing kindness all these years, do you ever feel that you've done enough? I mean, what makes you continue looking for new people who could use some kindness?"

Christopher answered simply and humbly: "Doing this makes me feel better about myself as a person." Whenever he catches himself reverting back to more self-centered habits, his priority of helping people serves to remind him of what's important.

We are so lucky to have Charleen and Christopher in our world to remind us of the healing power of kindness. It's never too late to channel kindness. My life has also been transformed by acts of kindness—both receiving and sharing. If you want to learn more about how to be a catalyst for kindness, join our #BeKind21 campaign, and be sure to visit our friends at the Random Acts of Kindness Foundation.

Lady Gaga

By the time we said good-bye and I offered my heartfelt thanks to Christopher for his gift and his wisdom, I realized that something in me had shifted. My grief over my loss was not entirely gone, of course, but I had begun to consider how I could do something kind for someone else who might be hurting. What a powerful feeling!

As I learned that day, being on the receiving end of a random act of kindness from a total stranger who's paying it forward can change your whole outlook on the world and the people in it.

Being one of the people Christopher helped, I witnessed for myself the value of kindness and how it can make us feel hope enough to trust again—knowing there are everyday individuals all around us who really do care. This is a feeling that, I believe, has the power to truly change the world.

Performing an act of kindness can redeem and heal you just as much as it can transform the person you choose to help.

Christopher's gift showed me the power that each one of us has to change a stranger's day and the world as a whole by channeling kindness and paying it forward, one kind act at a time.

THE COURAGE TO BE KIND TO YOURSELF

ALEXIS LEHRMAN

2

Life at fourteen years old is . . . let's just say . . . *confusing*! Our hormones are raging. That's tough enough to handle. What's worse is that this is the time when we become super-preoccupied with worries about *what others think of us*. As I learned the summer before ninth grade, when I went to sleepaway camp, this is often the age when some of us start "peacocking." Basically, that term refers to showing off or acting and dressing a certain way to look more attractive—all in the hopes of gaining favor with the cool kids.

Others? Well, we just try to survive. Trying to figure out who we are and where we fit in.

At camp that summer I met Andrew Kohn, a fellow rising freshman silently struggling with his identity. At six foot seven inches, Andrew was hard to miss. Though he didn't seem to have any interest in peacocking, fading into the background was clearly not an option.

Andrew quickly became known as the BFG (Big Friendly Giant). And *friendly* could not be a more appropriate description. Unfailingly kind and considerate, he was every camp kid's go-to goofball. Everyone at camp knew Andrew. Yet, as he later confided in me, most of the time he felt alone in his secret struggle to know who he was himself.

Although we had different interests and weren't alike in a lot of respects, the one thing we definitely had in common was a sense of humor. He could make me laugh like nobody else. And vice versa.

During the following school year, we kept in constant contact and grew even closer. Before long, he became my true friend and closest confidant. At the same time, even though Andrew had always been liberal in his compliments to me, he managed to avoid really talking about himself. After a series of failed efforts to get him to open up, I started to wonder, *Maybe I'm not being a good friend?* Then, in a brief flirtation with vanity, a new question arose: *Could Andrew possibly have a little crush on me?* After all, he did always seem to be holding something back.

Over the next summer at camp and the start of our sophomore year in high school, my questions were forgotten. At least, they were until one weekend early in the school year when, for the first time ever, Andrew turned the conversation to an apparently forbidden topic: himself.

Moments before, we'd been hanging out and having lunch at our favorite burger joint . . . chatting about *me*, of course. Then, as he finished the last of the fries, Andrew suddenly looked at me and calmly announced, "There's something I need to tell you."

There's something I need to tell you.

I waited.

He paused for a beat, composing himself before continuing, "I'm gay."

Before I could even think how best to respond, I blurted out, "When did you know?"

The story Andrew next related was not at all what I expected, nor was the wisdom he had attained as the result of an arduous journey of self-discovery—one I doubt any of us realized he was on.

Unlike his male friends, Andrew's repeated attempts at liking girls kept failing. He admitted, "I kept trying because I didn't want to be different."

In fact, one of his toughest obstacles early on had been overcoming the shame connected to what it would mean to be *different*. That's what had kept him from talking about his struggles—even with me. He was afraid of the truth, it seemed, until he could no longer ignore it.

The turning point had come during our previous summer at camp, when he and a small group of fellow campers embarked on a ten-day journey through the woods of North Carolina. In this Outward Bound–type program, they set out together with nothing but what they could carry on their backs. The most harrowing part of the trek is a twenty-four-hour solo stretch, where Andrew was on his own. Though Andrew knew the experience would be intense, he had no idea it would also be a defining moment in his life.

"The second I was on my own, it began pouring rain. Unfamiliar sounds surrounded me."

Was he freaked out?

In one word, Andrew answered: "Terrified."

He had spent so much time staying focused on friends and their issues that he'd managed to avoid looking at himself, other than occasionally wishing that his life was less complicated. Now that he was finally alone, that was about to change.

"When I couldn't distract myself with anyone else, I was forced to face what I didn't love about me. Not just what *it* was but also why I felt so sad about it." Alone on the trail, Andrew had no choice but to take a hard look at the experiences that might explain why he associated something bad with being gay. "I had to relive my life leading up to that moment."

There had been an incident in a floor hockey game in sixth grade that began when a player accused Andrew of fouling him. "Later on, in the locker room, the kid yelled at me, calling me weird and gay like it was an insult. I burst into tears after."

School then became just a place to conform, mainly because he was scared of being singled out again. "I thought I was different, and different was no good. I didn't want to be gay. I didn't want to have to worry about this issue, so I denied it. I tried to go after girls, but no matter how cute they were, I just wasn't attracted to them. And I just became more and more sad. I felt deprived of the things other kids my age had. I wanted to love myself and for someone to love me."

As he began to consider what he denied himself for fear of rejection, Andrew reached an emotional clearing in the woods. It resounded in his awareness: There were things he couldn't change.

"I am gay, I cannot change that, and I can't force people to accept me. I can only be me. And not accepting myself won't change anything or help anyone . . . including me."

These weren't totally new thoughts for Andrew. Yet, as he told me, those twenty-four hours of solitude allowed him, for the first time, to dig down deep enough to believe and accept that being gay was—and is—part of his true identity. Instead of dismissing his truth, he needed the courage to be a BFG toward himself. This revelation led to his resolve to not judge himself, to love himself enough to know, no matter what, that who he truly is can never be wrong.

This act of self-kindness allowed him to stand up, face the forest, and finally say the words "I am gay" out loud and embrace them. With those words came a taste of a life free from judgment and full of kindness offered to himself.

Alexis, thank you for sharing Andrew's story; and he's so right and brave—who we truly are can never be wrong. The path to finding out who that is can be bumpy—it was for me—and a friend can be so helpful in navigating that journey. If you're struggling with coming out or hoping to learn how to support someone who has come out, check out our friends at the It Gets Better Project or The Trevor Project.

Lady Gaga

The hours on his solo trek flew by from that point on. Gone was the silent dread tugging at his core. In fact, he told me, "I couldn't stop smiling." And if there is one thing I can tell you about an Andrew Kohn smile, it's that it is highly contagious.

Once he returned to civilization, friends, and school, he reclaimed his position as the center of fun, like the sun rising after a chilly night, casting warm rays of friendliness on those around him. Only now, he didn't hold back. Accepting who he was made him happy, and that happiness was reflected in every life he touched.

Getting there took courage. As his friend, being able to observe this shift in Andrew was the best gift he could have ever given me. Because of Andrew, I've learned sometimes the person who needs your kindness the most, is yourself.

The more I watch Andrew interact with others, secure in the knowledge of who he is, the more I think about what peacocks really do and why we should all do it a little more: They strut their true feathers.

3

THE GIFT OF BEING SEEN AND HEARD

THERESA STIER

Coffee. That's my cup of kindness of choice.

There are times when nothing can get me out of bed and out the door faster than anticipating the warmth and comfort of my preferred hot beverage. It's one of the many little things helping me survive college—especially 8:00 a.m. classes!

As I pull up a barstool at the Starbucks counter and wait for my order, it occurs to me that other simple forms of kindness can be offered even by someone who hasn't had their coffee yet . . . like holding the door open. Believe it or not, that smallest of gestures can start someone's day off better instead of worse.

In fact, earlier this particular morning, a groggy-looking stranger had paused to hold the door open for me. We had a quick exchange of "Thank you so much" and "You're welcome . . ." and that was all it took to put a pre-coffee glow on my face. Then, as I ordered my usual, "Skim latte with two pumps of sugar-free vanilla, please," my day was brightened enough for me to confess to the barista, "Or as I like to call it, the 'Kate Beckett.'" (If you get the reference to the TV series *Castle*, where the love of java plays a recurring role, you get an extra gold star.)

So once I grab my latte, because I'm earlier than usual, instead of rushing off to class I decide to sit there at the counter and savor my coffee. The decision proves to be a lucky one, because I wouldn't have wanted to miss the exchange about to unfold.

When I first notice the woman walking past me join the line to place her order, I can see that she is really anxious. Feeling like that's none of my business, though, I turn my attention away from her and back to my notes from my Russian class. But I can't avoid hearing the anxious tap-tapping of her heels against the tile floor. And when I overhear someone in line speaking to her, I can't help listening in.

This fellow is just making small talk—something about how the weather is nicer than it normally is in February—and before long, as they chat, the tapping of her shoes stops. One of the things she has mentioned to him is that she is on her way to a job interview and is extremely nervous. She admits, "I've been battling my anxiety since I woke up this morning, but I can't let all that self-doubt stop me."

When it's her turn to order, the man who has been talking to her for the last five minutes insists on paying for her tea. Before she can refuse his thoughtfulness, he adds, "Good luck with the interview!"

As I watch her place her order, then take the tea and make her way to the exit, I'm amazed to see that she is no longer the same anxious woman who'd walked past me a mere fifteen minutes earlier. Instead, I see someone confident and eager to embrace the day ahead.

That man who bought her tea was probably just getting himself a coffee before work, but he somehow showed up at just the right time to be there for this woman—at a moment when she didn't even know she needed his honest-to-goodness kindness. The free drink was nice, but what was truly kind was how he distracted her from her nervous thoughts, letting her know "You're going to do great!"

What if we all took his example? What if we ask someone we see pacing whether they are okay? What if, when we see an elderly person drop something, we pick it up for her? What if we help someone carry their grocery bags to their car because their three-year-old is throwing a temper tantrum? If, instead of just being onlookers, we all offer simple, small gestures in everyday, anxiety-provoking situations, we can make a difference.

So if you ever see someone who seems to be a little nervous, be the guy at Starbucks and start a conversation. Anxiety is real, and it's not just all in your head. But also, don't be offended if the person you'd like to help turns you down. Remember that coping with anxiety—or any variety of its sometimes-debilitating symptoms—can be tricky. According to the Anxiety and Depression Association of America (ADAA), anxiety is the most common mental illness in the US, affecting 40 million adults (ages eighteen and older), or 18 percent of the population. The ADAA also states that out of those 40 million people, only a third will seek treatment.

Sometimes we feel powerless to help others. However, as I'm sitting, packing up my books, and sipping the last of my coffee, I'm struck by how powerful it can be to simply listen to someone else's concerns and, most of all, to let them know they've been heard and seen.

Me too, Theresa, me too. Coffee is kindness in my life. I love the story you shared that accompanied your early morning coffee, and I love the lesson you're sharing with us. We can and should try to take notice of the needs and feelings of the people around us, whether it's a smile at the anxious woman in the coffee line or holding a door open for the frazzled parent pushing the stroller. These small actions can mean a lot, and your story shows that they do. We encourage you to pay the kindness forward and perform three acts of kindness in your community. If you need help getting started, check out Youth Service America for ideas.

Lady Gaga

This is the conclusion I take with me out in the mild winter morning—that you never know how much you might be able to help someone else just by taking the time to really see them and, perhaps, by offering a few well-timed, kind words.

4

Score a Friend

HANNA ATKINSON

The first time I ever heard the phrase "inclusive friendships" was on an otherwise uneventful day in high school. It was uttered by a fellow student, Sarah Greichen, an amazing person who I soon learned embodies that phrase more than anyone I've ever met.

Let me set the scene.

In the large cafeteria, I was sitting alone, eating my lunch.

As a young girl with Down syndrome, that happened to me often. No stranger to loneliness, most of the time I managed to keep a smile on my face—not wanting anyone to think I felt sorry for myself. Maybe I did so in the hope that someone would feel comfortable enough to plunk down beside me one day. Sarah turned out to be that someone, and as we began to converse, we quickly discovered that we were both on the high school swim and dive team. She was also becoming a member of the Youth Activation Committee (YAC) for Special Olympics of Colorado, a committee I'd been on for a while. It's a group that plans activities for Special Olympics athletes and for young partners who are not intellectually disabled, like Sarah. She was joining with her twin brother, Jacob, who has an autism spectrum disorder.

"Oh, a twin," I said, recalling the magic I'd always associated with being a twin. Without being too nosy, I asked her what growing up as part of a duo had been like for her.

When they were young it was wonderful, Sarah said, telling me they'd been born only two minutes apart and were always close. But as the two of them started school and began to socialize, she noticed differences between her and Jacob that broke her heart. "Everything was harder for him than it was for me, whether it was getting ready for the day, communicating with people, or doing schoolwork," Sarah said. Watching him struggle with things that were out of his control

inspired her to want to help. "From a very young age, I became his advocate and his best friend." For the most part, Jacob was a genuinely happy kid, and Sarah always managed to cheer him up if he was having a tough day.

"Always?"

Well, she admitted, as long as they were in the same classes. When a decision had been made to place Jacob in a separate special education classroom, he began to regress. Once that happened, she said, "People began to see Jacob as his diagnosis, which is not who he is! And by the middle of that year, he came home crying and just lost it." Their mom tried to comfort him, and all he could say was, "I have no friends. Why don't I have any friends?"

Without meaning to interrupt, I had to say, "That's so unfair!" Maybe Sarah could see that I'd experienced my own low points.

She went on. "High school was even worse for Jacob. Halfway through ninth grade, he stopped talking completely."

After watching him change over the years from that happy kid who felt included in everything to feeling constantly depressed and isolated, Sarah grew more and more frustrated. "You're right," she said. "It was unfair. For twins born two minutes apart with a lot in common, the difference in our lives was huge. I was in strong academic classes, I had friends, I had sports and activities, and I was happy. Seeing that I had all of that and he didn't made me angry and made me want to change it."

Wow, I thought, *that's how to deal with anger—choose to channel it into action to change the status quo. But* how?

"My goal from the start," Sarah explained, "was to create something that would change things not only for Jacob but also for other kids who struggle with isolation and not having any friends." She began with the awareness that students usually make friends through academic classes, sports, and after-school organizations. That same year in the ninth grade, when she was still only thirteen years old, Sarah struck upon the idea of an "inclusion club"—one that would welcome all individuals with different talents and abilities. She hoped such a club could give Jacob the chance to connect with other students.

Sarah sincerely believed that if other kids knew Jacob in the way she knew him, they would love to be his friend.

"I have always seen Jacob for who he really is," she said. "He loves to play the Wii, he's smart, he has an incredible sense of humor, he loves Harry Potter, he loves any action-adventure movie, he loves to color, he loves to be with people, and he loves when people challenge him to be the greatest version of himself."

Her model for creating a new club was partly inspired by some of the unified sports programs run by Special Olympics that pair students with disabilities with those who are not disabled. Sarah's concept for inclusion was to go beyond athletics by connecting people with one another for the purpose of creating friendships. When she presented her idea to officials at Special Olympics, they loved and supported her vision. Soon after, she created a Score A Friend club model to be used in schools for students of all ages, from elementary to college.

In a short amount of time, Score A Friend—born to promote and support the inclusion of students of all abilities in schools and communities—became a reality. On the day back in 2014 when I first met Sarah, I was amazed to learn how her idea had been embraced by school administrators and students alike. She described to me how members worked together to address issues impacting students and to find ways to advocate for them. Members could interact with one another in unified sports and unified elective courses, as well as team up with organizations that offer opportunities for community service. Not only were the clubs building inclusive friendships; they were also creating a wave of activists.

Sometimes great ideas by young idealists can gain traction only to lose momentum down the road. Not so for Score A Friend, and I was glad to hear it after recently touching base with Sarah. What started out as a way to channel her anger into something positive—with the goal to simply find her brother a friend—has now snowballed into a much larger, lifelong mission.

"To me, helping others is by far the most fulfilling thing anyone can do," Sarah told me. "Anyone can make a difference, even if it is just one small act."

In many ways, these clubs highlight the pure kindness and acceptance that many people long for.

"Inclusion to me is just walking up to someone and being yourself," Sarah said. **"Being inclusive is having a human connection without placing judgments before it."** At nineteen years old, she had concluded that inclusion, friendship, and kindness all go hand in hand.

Her example has shown me what it means to be a good friend—being there for someone, getting to know them for who they truly are, never judging, and being both kind and honest. I'll never forget Sarah's other insights, that

> *"Being a kind and respectful friend includes opening your mind to other perspectives, pushing yourself to understand someone else even if you haven't experienced the same things, and committing yourself to being there in a supportive capacity."*

As for the club Sarah created, Score A Friend is now a nonprofit with chapters undergoing development all across the United States. It is an organization that channels all the possibilities that kindness and community can bring about.

One of those possibilities is that a lonely young girl with Down syndrome might Score A Friend for life. After all, that's what happened with me and my now-best friend, Sarah Greichen.

♥

Hannah, thank you for sharing your best friend with us! I am so moved by Sarah's comment that she wanted to improve Jacob's circumstances, of course, and I'm also incredibly touched that she wanted to make sure that no one else ever felt isolated or lonely. This is true about each and every young person I've had the pleasure of meeting—they want to solve problems for themselves, for their friends, and for people they would never, ever meet. Sarah's vision for Score A Friend is beautiful, hopeful, and kind—just as she is—and I'm elated to hear of the club's growth. For more information on how to build a more inclusive community, check out Score A Friend or Best Buddies International, and don't forget to commit to inclusiveness by signing the Special Olympics Inclusion Pledge!

Lady Gaga

THE KINDNESS OF

no matter how unfair or discouraging the world may seem at certain points, kindness is actually abundant at all times

OFFERING ACCESS

5 TAYLOR M. PARKER

By way of introduction, my name is Taylor M. Parker and, as of this writing, I'm a college student at Indiana University–Purdue University Indianapolis (IUPUI). *Everyday philanthropist* is the best term to describe what I do and why I care.

There are many areas of the community in which I serve. One area in particular is a concern I'm most passionate about. Whenever I'm asked what it was that sparked my interest, I usually respond, "I don't know if there was any one specific experience that made me realize people deserve humanity."

That answer lies at the heart of why I am most passionate about my work as a menstrual hygiene access activist.

Let's face it: Given the social stigma, conversation around the need for menstrual hygiene access is essentially nonexistent. To some, merely speaking about menstruation in a public setting is viewed as radical or even taboo; to others who may simply be unaware of the need in the first place, the subject is still seen as TMI.

This is the climate in which my passion grows. After all, is it really Too Much Information to talk about the cost associated with menstrual hygiene products, or to ask, for example, *Did you know that, for every person who menstruates, the cost is at the very least $7 a month?* If you do the math and extend that to $84 a year for forty years (the average length a person will menstruate), then you're talking about thousands of dollars—an expense far too many cannot afford.

If even that seems hard to imagine, almost all of us who menstruate, regardless of our age, can recall that feeling of panic we had, or a friend has had, when we, or they, forgot to bring a tampon "just in case" that day. Now imagine living with that fear—always. That is the reality for people all around us—coworkers, classmates, friends, and family. More often than not, the people directly impacted by this inaccessibility will not bring up their plight in everyday conversation; they will struggle in silence.

Those who do bravely speak out on this issue are often overlooked and pushed aside, most of the time because of the unfortunate fact that people are generally uncomfortable with the topic.

There was a time, I admit, when I took access for granted. Early in 2015, however, during my junior year of high school, that changed when I was approached by a friend after class who asked, "Do you have five dollars you can spare for me to buy a box of tampons?"

As someone who had already gained a reputation for being an approachable, open-minded advocate for other students, I was quick to say, "Absolutely," and I bought her a box—only for her to come to me again a month later with the same request.

This time my friend confided in me, providing more context for her situation. Her father, her family's only source of income, had been laid off, and her family couldn't afford groceries, let alone tampons for her and the other women in her household.

In a position to help, each month I continued to buy menstrual products for her and her other family members—until her dad found another job and the family was able to get back on its feet. In the meantime, I became awakened to economic inequalities in so many communities, leading me to see just how pervasive the need was—and how inaccessible these very necessary products are.

Claire Coder, the founder of Aunt Flow—a for-profit company that stocks business and school bathrooms with freely accessible 100% organic cotton tampons and pads—said it best when she stated, "Menstrual products are not a luxury. Yet, they are not covered by food stamps or WIC (Women, Infants and Children program), and are taxed in many states. No one should ever be forced to choose between food and tampons."

As obvious as those points might seem, from the moment my eyes were opened to the urgency of the issue, I was also confronted with the challenge of getting past the social stigma surrounding menstruation. Without conversation, how else could others' eyes be opened?

Flash forward to November 5, 2017, about two and a half years after my friend first approached me with her predicament. It was on that night, as I stood outside of Bankers Life Fieldhouse in Indianapolis, Indiana, watching excited ticket holders arrive for a Lady Gaga concert that I witnessed the answer to my question.

In planning my first large-scale menstrual product drive, I had been given the support of Lady Gaga's Born This Way Foundation, along with that of Peace First—a nonprofit dedicated to helping young people around the world become powerful and effective peacemakers. When next puzzling over how to get the word out about the drive, I'd been blown away to hear from executives at the venue and at mega-promoter Live Nation. They told me that, a week before the concert, they would share my mission on media channels and include a call to action for fans and ticket holders; they could get involved by bringing a donation to the concert.

And that's how you create conversation—you get informed, become an advocate, engage partners, and, hopefully, inspire others. Clearly, there is power in numbers when it comes to tackling social stigmas. That said, I had no idea how our best-laid plans would turn out.

The response was unbelievable! I will never forget the thrill of watching thousands of excited fans stride up to our drop-off table with handfuls, armfuls, bags, and boxes of donations. What had begun as a small purchase of one box of tampons between friends grew into a massive collection that yielded upward of six thousand menstrual products—on that night alone.

Before the newly inspired activists hurried off, I had the chance to ask some of them, "What motivated you to donate to this drive?" The responses varied:

"I know how scary it is not to have these when I need them. I want to help someone."

"I didn't realize this was an issue, but I knew I had to do something about it when I found out."

Most of the answers were similar . . . although one was pretty unique:

"I would do anything for Gaga, and if she tells me to give, I'll give. She knows what she's about. She knows kindness."

In those moments of connecting to fans with big hearts from all backgrounds, there were more than a few lessons for me, including the truth that **no matter how unfair or discouraging the world may seem at certain points, kindness is actually abundant at all times**.

Over the next several days, I saw further proof of why it matters when celebrities use their massive platforms to raise awareness about issues that are being ignored. Thanks to the involvement of Born This Way and Peace First, we were able to collect and give away more than 6,700 menstrual hygiene products and 450 clothing items to be distributed to students in need, specifically low income, LGBTQ+, and women students on our campus. Our drive also directly benefited more than a hundred IUPUI students, faculty, and staff. On the IUPUI campus, I'm keeping the momentum going, connecting to other campuses to ignite an advocacy campaign around the country.

Yes, it's not easy to get the conversation going at first, but there are numerous ways you can take action to get involved. For starters, you might contact your local homeless and women's shelters to learn about their donation process and how you can make menstrual hygiene access a reality for the people they serve.

If you don't have the means to donate, spread the word to your friends and family and simply broach the subject.

If you are matter-of-fact, informed, and compassionate, your concern about lack of access can become contagious. Learn about the problem. Give to those in need. Share the passion with others. Support those also doing the work.

There's always a way to help others gain access, whatever their obstacles and regardless of what resources you may or may not have, and there's always an opportunity to channel kindness—through the smallest efforts that enrich your life as much as they do others'.

My prediction is that once you choose to become an everyday philanthropist, you will never look back.

♥

The term *everyday philanthropist* is everything, Taylor. How much better would our world be if people thought about how to meet others' needs, every day? I didn't know that the cost of menstruation is at least $7 per month—what a privilege it is to never have had to think about that cost; everyone deserves that peace of mind. We're so appreciative of Taylor for recognizing a need in their community and organizing their peers around a cause that made such a significant difference in the lives of hundreds of individuals. We encourage you to follow Taylor's lead and start your own drive, and if you or someone you know is in need of menstrual products or would like to donate menstrual products, please visit PERIOD or call 211, a free, confidential referral and information helpline.

Lady Gaga

6

HAVING CAKE AND SHARING IT, TOO

HANA MANGAT

Whenever we hear impressive stories about social entrepreneurs who channel kindness by creating a start-up enterprise aimed at solving social problems or effecting social change, often the assumption is that they've come up with an original idea that no one's ever developed before. The truth is that, in order to channel kindness, you don't have to reinvent the wheel or do something that's totally original.

You can always join in someone else's movement and, if you want, add your own twist. You can always take a page out of someone else's book and write your own version.

In 2015, that's exactly what fifteen-year-old Allison Wachen and her brother Robert of Montgomery County, Maryland, decided to do. Allison, a high school student at the time, happened to be flipping through a magazine when an article about a national charity called Birthday Cakes 4 Free (BC4F) caught her attention. The story about this non-profit inspired Allison to start her own local chapter. She loved the basic mission of volunteer groups in every community getting together to "bake, decorate, and deliver free birthday cakes for financially and socially disadvantaged children and seniors."

The part of the article that really grabbed Allison was its recognition that, no matter what the scope of the birthday celebration, time-old tradition gives us this one day every year when we experience the magical combination of candles being blown out and the singing of a familiar melody as we wish for whatever our hearts desire. She hadn't realized before learning of BC4F how many people, young and old, lack the resources or capacity to have a birthday cake of their own on their special day. That just didn't sit right with her.

Starting a local chapter made all the sense in the world to Allison. It was a perfect way, she thought, to combine her baking talent with her passion for community service. Better yet, when her younger brother Robert expressed an interest in getting on board as her chapter cofounder and vice president of technology, and their cousin Sawyer asked to help, too, she was even more energized by the family fun to be had. They went to work immediately to get BC4F of Montgomery County off the ground—for children of every age.

HANA MANGAT

Once their friends heard about the endeavor, they happily volunteered. Allison began by organizing cake-baking and -decorating socials once a month with kids from the local middle school and high school. She was so impressed by their commitment that she decided to make the organization completely student-run—from the executive board on down.

That's how Allison took a page from something others had started, added her own twist, and wrote her own version.

In a little over two years, as Allison later told reporters from ABC News, her chapter's membership went from a sprinkling of kids to more than four hundred members. They went from delivering ten cakes a month to a hundred. Today, out of the sixty-four chapters across the United States, BC4F of Montgomery County, Maryland, is the largest and only student-run chapter in the country.

None of it happened overnight. Allison recalls that people initially assumed that, because it was a youth-driven organization just starting out, they might not be so organized. That changed once they got a few takers and word of mouth spread rapidly about how delicious and beautiful the cakes were and, more importantly, how joyful their donated birthday cakes made the recipients and their guests feel. Along with that reputation for excellence came word-of-mouth about how well-organized they actually were.

As her chapter's cofounder and president, Allison has long encouraged her volunteers to decorate each cake as its own individual work of art. Her familiar refrain is "Make this cake as if you were giving it to someone in your family."

Taking that a step further, the student volunteers make a concerted effort to be present not just to deliver the birthday cakes but to witness the reaction of those in attendance. Their kindness is usually acknowledged with such heartfelt gratitude that they are all the more inspired. Sometimes there's that one person who's speechless—like the child who wrote them a thank-you note later, saying, "Wow! A cake with my name on it! I've never seen one with my name before." There is general consensus from all the recipients that their own birthday cakes make them feel valued by the entire community. One little girl commented in amazement, "And they don't even know us." Another said, "It's nice they do this for other kids, too."

The BC4F student volunteers have been known to visit with recipients after the birthday celebration is over. At an event at the Greentree Shelter in Bethesda, Maryland, members lingered to speak with a group of fifteen adults for almost three hours, curious to know and understand more about their experiences, opinions, and lives. Inspiration, compassion, and frosting floated all around.

Aliya Klein, the secretary of BC4F of Montgomery County, explains the significance of the cakes themselves: "A birthday cake is a symbol for celebration, and since the celebration of life is extremely important, I think everyone should have the opportunity to receive one on their birthday."

Now in college, Allison has handed the reins of the organization to her brother Robert and cousin Sawyer, and is confident that the team's efforts will flourish in their well-trained hands. While they're in charge now, she still points out that for their BC4F chapter to continue to grow, public donations are always appreciated—especially because of the high cost of cake-decorating supplies and especially the cake-delivery containers.

Allison's conviction that a basic blueprint for a charity could be put into action and run by youth has paid off, something that has empowered her immeasurably. "Simply put, my involvement in BC4F shaped my high school experience by giving me confidence that I can be a leader who can make a difference in my community." The chapter's collective success is concrete evidence that young people can make a meaningful impact in their communities.

Although the national organization of the BC4F dissolved in 2019, the BC4F is its own 501c(3) nonprofit organization and titled Birthday Cakes 4 Free Maryland. As of March 2020, BC4F has donated 5,638 cakes to 23 charities in the DC Metropolitan area, and the organization has over 750 volunteers. This wonderful nonprofit is full of dedicated, passionate individuals who are helping spread love and joy in free-birthday-cake form, and some who are even real-life genies making wishes come true.

♥

Hana, you are so right. So many people think changing the world means you have to start your own organization and campaign, and while that's absolutely part of it sometimes, there is so much amazing work already happening. Let's learn about what exists—strengthen those efforts and help solve more problems. Check out Idealist and VolunteerMatch to learn more about the good things happening in our communities.

Lady Gaga

7

THE ART OF KINDNESS

NICHOLAS McCARDLE

Every picture tells a story.

That's one of the lessons that young artists are apt to discover whenever they gather for summer classes with their teacher, Claire Pittman, an artist and college student attending West Liberty University near Wheeling, West Virginia.

Claire—who grew up with a passion for art—is a believer in the power of self-expression and feels that it's important to cultivate creativity in others. Especially in young people. Even at a very young age, she could always be found creating a visual story. Abstract finger paintings, drawings of cartoon characters, still lifes, impressions of nature, people . . . you name it.

Art gave her an outlet and an escape from issues in her life and their emotional toll, which Claire learned to hide. Her sensitivity to whatever was going on, bad or good, and her identity as an artist made her feel different, somehow separate and apart from others—which led to her being frequently singled out. The discomfort of feeling "other than" or "less than" also became something Claire tried to hide. She figured that if she was being called out for her sensitive personality in general, it would only make it worse to show her passion for art.

Yet as time went on, she found ways to turn those perceived negatives into true positives. "Funny enough, what I was hiding would ultimately bring me out into the light," Claire said.

"And being different would be what makes me, well, me."

The journey toward embracing herself and one of her biggest inspirations for artwork began in her grandfather's sunflower garden. As a little girl, she used to revel in the beauty of the towering plants. Each year, her grandfather would cut the sunflowers down for her and her sister to use as walking sticks, and sometimes, she'd pick apart the petals to press into books.

To this day, her grandfather still has a sunflower garden, and Claire visits regularly to take photographs that inspire new visual stories to tell. "Those sunflowers were such a crucial part of my childhood," she notes with a fond twinkle in her eyes, "and I long for those times."

Another meaningful influence was her own art teacher in school—who she feels was responsible for helping broaden her mind to see the world, herself, and her art in a whole new light. During a summer internship, her mentor also opened a door that led to Claire's first teaching experience. Through this, she was able to realize the extent of her compassion and patience for children, and her understanding of them.

Everything became clear: Her calling as an artist was to work with kids. But where could she begin to pursue that path? When the answer came to her—to start with the fun of hosting summer art classes in her home—Claire thought, *Why not?* and decided to drop a few mentions on social media to pique interest. After gaining some inquiries, she got right to work on organizing classes. Her hope was twofold: 1) To plant an appreciation of art in her students; and 2) To introduce them to the craft of expressing themselves as individuals.

"Self-expression is human nature," Claire says. "To open children up at an early age and to keep them open through the years with art . . . that is a wonderful thing."

Proving the *Field of Dreams* adage, "If you build it, they will come," she soon had a group of students signed up, raring to go. For the first class, and those that followed, the session began with Claire welcoming every kid into her home. The group gathered around her kitchen table, where she engaged them in simple, open conversation. They were able to share how their days were going, how they were spending their summers, and any stories they wanted to tell. Claire cherished the warmth and freeflow of the exchanges, finding genuine enjoyment in listening to her students.

Next, as she had planned, the group easily slid right into that day's art project. Claire worked along with them, guiding and giving instruction. Her goal was to encourage and never to criticize, always making sure every young artist was given their own creative freedom. After projects were complete, it was snack time!

Pleased with the structure after a few days of having class up and running, Claire had to say, "It's such a wonderful routine. I wish we could do it every single day!"

The lessons learned were many. Claire feels that whether the stories shared in conversation suggested ideas for artwork or the pictures produced by the artwork inspired stories, it didn't matter. What counted was the happy experience shared with one another in its making. The bonds that Claire and her students made over the course of that summer were her biggest reward. She loved hearing and telling stories and getting to know all about each student, right down to their favorite colors, most beloved hobbies, even their hopes, worries, dreams, and goals. Without saying it in so many words, she felt the kids realized they could have a teacher who might have been a lot like them when she was their age.

More than anything, Claire says she is forever grateful for those kids who stuck with her through her program's first flight and who gave her the chance to do what she loves. Their discoveries further inspired her, firing her up with an even greater passion for art and the opportunity to teach it.

Without question, that inspiration goes two ways. Claire's hope is that as she moves forward as an art teacher, her current and former students will continue to love art in general and to love making it themselves. With the new perspectives she was able to show them, she further hopes they'll flourish not only on their artistic journeys, but also in their growth as communicators and as warmhearted, kind human beings.

For all who have a talent, passion, or calling, why not follow Claire's example by choosing to share your knowledge with those in your community, perhaps by offering classes?

The more we share our stories—through words or pictures, music or drama—the kinder our world will be.

♥

Wow, how beautiful. I especially love Claire's comment that what she was hiding would ultimately bring her into the light. I've had that same experience and art has been absolutely healing for me. You're right, Nicholas, self-expression is so important and art is one of the many ways you can express your feelings. Your art matters. What you have to say matters. If you'd like to explore the many ways art can help you, a friend, or your child, check out The Dreaming Zebra Foundation or Art Feeds, as well as local resources in your communities.

Lady Gaga

8

KINDNESS
in
SPORTS

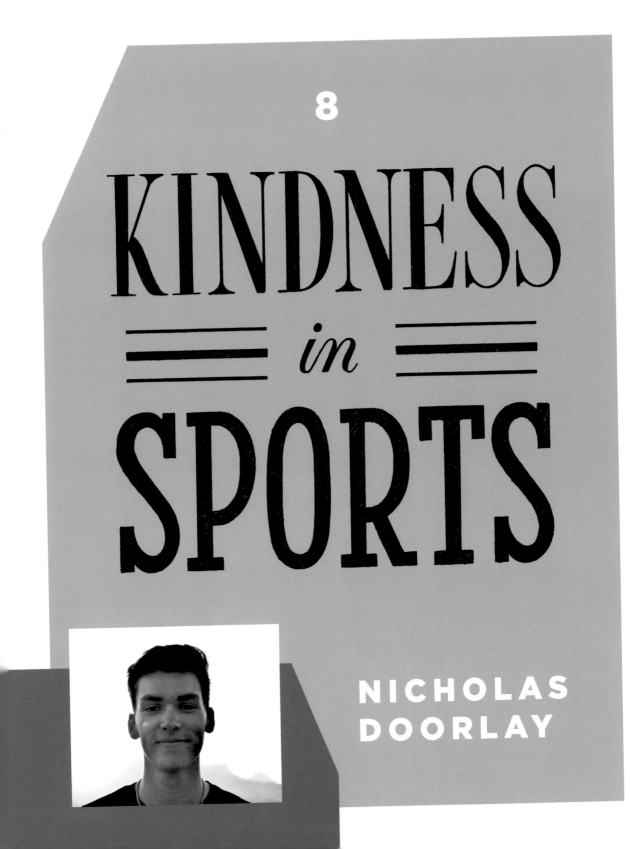

NICHOLAS
DOORLAY

To a lot of male athletes and their fans, kindness is *uncool*. On high school football fields and basketball courts, that reality is embedded in the macho, combative culture of the game. It's also reflected in the fights and bouts vividly seen in most major sports leagues—from the NFL to the NBA, NHL, MLB, and so on. In boxing, wrestling, mixed martial arts, and other such matchups, the battles and the language are all about brute force and are aimed at completely debilitating your opponent.

Athletes, competitive by nature, may be prone to allowing their tempers to flare. They may even lose their cool on purpose if it can give them an advantage. Hey, they're just out there trying to win. You can't blame them. It's as simple as that.

But what if it's *not* as simple as that? Wild idea, right? At least, it seemed that way to me, up until the end of my freshman year of high school. Though I'd grown up playing every sport imaginable, once I started the ninth grade, my choice had been to focus on baseball. The expectation had been that I'd play all four years.

However, after that first season, I'd had enough. Within our own team and the other teams in our league, the negative energy seemed pronounced. In my experience, no one was very kind, and it was a little too cutthroat out there, especially for freshman baseball.

In my sophomore winter season, when I drifted toward basketball, a sport that, at six feet six inches, I hoped might be a better fit, it was the same deal. How disappointing to confront this perception that somehow being kind, compassionate, and concerned about someone else was a sign of weakness. Though I loved the sport, I was distraught by the dog-eat-dog, every-player-for-themselves atmosphere, and I could not handle being around it for hours at a time.

With spring rapidly approaching, I worried that maybe my days as a high school athlete were numbered. That was when I was convinced to try out for track and field. With some trepidation, I decided to give it a shot.

This third attempt at finding the right sport immediately proved to be the charm. No longer a misfit, I felt like this was where I'd belonged from the start. Kind of like the story of the ugly duckling, who didn't know he was actually a swan all along. The sport itself hooked me the minute I joined and hasn't let me go since. Better yet, the members of the team got along with one another and were unapologetically kind. And at my first meet, much to my happy surprise, I witnessed the fact that, in this athletic contest, *everyone* is your friend.

In no way are track and field athletes seen as weak or lesser competitors. At track meets, I have met more kind people than anywhere else in my life. At first I had to ask if there was an explanation, if perhaps the sport managed to just attract people of extreme kindness. Maybe that is partly the case, but I quickly realized what was actually happening: In the atmosphere of track, **it is *cool* to be kind**. In such a setting that recognizes the coolness of kindness, you also recognize the true nature of being a champion and just how awesome people can be.

The big breaking news is that **when you are in an atmosphere where kindness becomes the norm, you realize that it is indeed possible to be competitive and kind at the same time**. Think of how cool this is: At one meet where twenty-six high jumpers were vying for the top seven spots in order to move on to section finals, every athlete out there was 100 percent supportive of the others and cheering everyone on. The same athletes I was getting ready to try to best were giving me tips and pointers.

Learning to see kindness as a strength is a lesson I believe will shape who I am and make me that much more formidable in life, as well as in track and field competitions. If you're in a sport or on a team that seems too cutthroat or aggressive, try leading by example and adopting an attitude of kindness. You may make a new friend. During my first track season, I made at least ten new friends from opposing schools alone. Instead of yelling at an opponent, give a pointer or cheer them on.

When I performed at Super Bowl LI, we brought kindness (in the form of Born This Way Foundation) to Houston, and with our partners at Mattel, we gave out more than 10,000 toys to local nonprofit organizations. Nicholas and I agree: kindness is cool and it definitely has a place in sports. His story is the perfect example of how we can bring kindness into any sport, activity, or hobby we engage in. The next time you play sports, either for fun or competition, we challenge you to practice good sportsmanship, and if you need some tips on how to get started, visit Good Sport Club or Playworks.

Lady Gaga

It's much easier to be competitive and kind than you think. And once you try that the first time, it's pretty hard to stop.

9

JESSICA ZHANG

KINDNESS CREATES COOL

Arizonans like to say that they manage to withstand their summers' brutal heat by insisting, well, that it's a *dry* heat—unlike other, much steamier and more humid parts of the country. Yet, dry or not, the truth is that not everyone can escape into the cooler confines of air-conditioned offices, homes, or cars or grab the chance to take a refreshing dip in a pool. And with temperatures often soaring to over 100 degrees Fahrenheit and sometimes lasting spans of weeks, the heat in cities like Phoenix has increasingly become intolerable for many and even life-threatening—with heat strokes and dehydration on the rise for the common resident.

Among the most vulnerable in the summer months are those experiencing homelessness—a problem that one man is passionately setting out to address.

Phoenix native Matthew Tees is a social entrepreneur whose business is named CART Mobile Convenience. Through CART, Matthew travels around downtown Phoenix, selling prepackaged food, drinks, and other miscellaneous items. Matthew sells his wares from his electric-powered golf cart, mostly at locations in and around Phoenix with stops primarily at office buildings, restaurants, and schools. For every water bottle he sells, he donates a water bottle, and for every food item he sells, he donates a food item.

His call to action came from two realizations in one day. The first, as he notes, was that in an instant-gratification society, most working people and others want immediate access to food and drinks as well. "I wanted to be able to provide those items to people who can't leave the office or job site," he says. The second realization was that the Phoenix community would want to support the less fortunate by patronizing a business trying to make a difference.

Matthew decided to make a bet on convenience and kindness.

After being approved by the city as a small mobile business, he went from having fifteen transactions the first day to selling more than 1,250 water bottles and three hundred food items within only a few months—then delivering those same quantities to those in need.

Matthew has a menu that is twofold: ever-evolving to accommodate the needs of his customers and help the community.

First off, busy downtown workers can support the small business and quickly grab a snack during a break. There is both variety and convenience associated with buying from CART. Secondly, Matthew helps deliver all the donated proceeds to benefit those impacted hardest by the extremely dry weather conditions and soaring temperatures.

Matthew greets all his customers with a contagious friendliness, always asking, "How's your day going today?" hoping to cheer them up with conversation, laughter, and food.

As to why he gives away equal numbers to what he sells, Matthew explains, "I am a downtown Phoenix resident, so I witness firsthand a lot of less-fortunate, forgotten-about people." It just makes sense that if he is building a business he would want a portion of his profits to go back to the neighborhood and all its residents. The "buy-one-give-one" approach of social entrepreneurships like TOMS Shoes and Warby Parker has proven to be a successful business model. Customers like knowing their dollars will go toward uplifting someone else and solving a growing social issue.

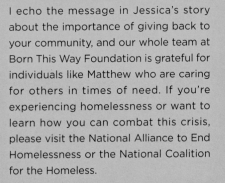

I echo the message in Jessica's story about the importance of giving back to your community, and our whole team at Born This Way Foundation is grateful for individuals like Matthew who are caring for others in times of need. If you're experiencing homelessness or want to learn how you can combat this crisis, please visit the National Alliance to End Homelessness or the National Coalition for the Homeless.

Lady Gaga

To that end, Matthew has become well-versed in the reality of the systemic problem of unequal access to water and food in the hot temperatures of Arizona. He likes his beneficiaries to feel as appreciated as his customers. "It is my goal to provide them with a cold bottle of water, a smile, and a kind, humane interaction—something they might not often get in their circumstances."

Many of his customers, who are fans of his dedication, become repeat supporters, asking him to frequent their workplaces by requesting deliveries. Matthew has a reputation for never forgetting a name and making sure to greet everyone with a hello and later a good-bye. This kind of individual customer service may be one reason he's drawn so much of the public—who usually avoid leaving their offices to face the outrageous temperatures—to go outside and visit CART.

Regular patron Marc praises Matthew, saying, "The service is excellent! Matt is scrupulously honest, endlessly helpful, and very creative about improvising on the fly."

When Matthew rolls up to interact with citizens who are experiencing homelessness, his hope is that they can see him as a source of aid. Never in a hurry, he'll talk with them at length, getting a sense of their lives and challenges and how he can continue to help.

One of Matthew's beneficiaries, Tony S., was able to thank him personally during a water and food drop-off. His message was simple: "Thank you for what you're doing. We really need this help. A lot of people just forget about us or don't care."

On the hottest days, Matthew drives along the roads and stops wherever he sees anyone who may need help, offering several bottles of ice-cold water. In more populated areas, such as public parks and bus stations, he parks the CART and walks around to deliver his goods to those who might be wary or who do not know he's legitimately offering help.

He admits, "Sometimes those interactions can be hard emotionally or harsh to witness, but that is the reality of their situations. I try to be a bright spot in their day, even if it is brief." As much as he encourages anyone he meets who is struggling, he acknowledges that the stories of those on the street or without basic resources have taught him about grit and resilience. Without a doubt, he says, "CART is a real learning experience daily, in every sense of the words."

Plans for expanding his operations are in the works. You can always continue to spread the love, Matthew believes. To combat the effects that the excessive heat levels have on all residents of Phoenix, he hopes to have even more carts in the near future to serve more people and a larger area.

In the meantime, Matthew Tees has proven that being an entrepreneur and a philanthropist can go hand in hand, and that success is ultimately defined by the size of your heart, not by the size of your bank account.

10

BICYCLE JOURNEYS OF HOPE

HANNA ATKINSON

"Summertime and the livin' is easy . . ." goes the old song from the opera *Porgy and Bess* (music by George Gershwin)—a standard from way, way back that's been around from long before most of us (or our parents for that matter) were alive. Even so, the feeling those words conjure is something we all recognize: the promise of summer, sun-filled days of freedom, and adventure that allows us to re-group, relax, and recharge.

For those of us who are students, summer might mean outdoor fun or traveling with friends, a family vacation, or maybe some form of internship, a full-fledged job, a research project, or an opportunity to volunteer for a great cause. The latter—with a focus on raising money and disability awareness—is an option for fraternity members of all chapters of Pi Kappa Phi. Along with life-changing experiences that take place while riding the route—aptly named the Journey of Hope—they're also able to enjoy the very best moments that summer has to offer.

Service, of course, is huge for most fraternities, and Pi Kappa Phi is no exception; in fact, it's the only national fraternity to run their own nonprofit. Launched in 1976 as a project to mobilize Pi Kappa Phi undergrads, The Ability Experience started out as a one-time opportunity to help with the construction of a therapeutic play unit for children with severe disabilities. From those modest beginnings, the nonprofit has since evolved into a model program with a powerful, ambitious vision to change public perception of people with disabilities. As the organizers point out,

---

"Disability doesn't mean inability. People with disabilities often have to do things a little differently."

However (unless you know someone personally or have someone in your family with a disability), you may not find it so easy to have empathy for that person's sit-uation, feelings, hopes, and fears. The Ability Experience made it a priority to create real change by providing various ways for volunteers and others to gain firsthand experience of the challenges faced by people with disabilities. In the process of doing so, it has also proven to be one of the most dramatic philanthropic successes among Greek organizations in the United States—raising more than $15 million for individuals with disabilities and the organizations that serve them!

Progress was slow in the '70s and early '80s. Then, in 1987, Pi Kappa Phi alumnus Bruce Rogers had a brainstorm about what he could do to gain more public awareness for The Ability Experience. He had been asking himself how he could do something small to make a meaningful difference—not only in how society views people with disabilities but also how they perceive fraternities.

If he could do something to make a little splash, he decided, that would give him a public platform to galvanize attention. So Bruce's big idea was to set off on a solo bike ride across America and use his stops to stir up conversations in communities that reflected the nonprofit's goal to "promote empathy over sympathy and work to open spaces, increase access, and promote inclusivity." He thought he could challenge the labels, language, and perceptions that are unfairly imposed on people with disabilities, as well as on fraternity members. Besides, alone out on the open road on his bicycle, facing the elements, viewing the beauty of unexplored places—he knew he would have a memorable summer adventure.

The very next year, Pi Kappa Phi formed a team of twenty to ride across the country. Even before the Internet and its ability to send thoughts around the world at the speed of light, word spread rapidly, as acts of kindness somehow found a way of catching on. The buzz began.

Now, just over thirty years after that initial ride, the Journey of Hope cross-country bicycle ride is made up of three teams, with about ninety cyclists in total. Each rider raises money for their trip as well as money for donations to organizations supporting people with disabilities. They start on the West Coast, in three locations—San Francisco, Los Angeles, and Seattle—and all end up in Washington, D.C., for a spectacular inclusive celebration.

Teams stop for planned "friendship visits" with invited members of the public and the disabled community. From bowling and pool parties to old-fashioned barbecues, the summer fun of the festivities give all a chance to relax, regroup, and recharge. Each incredible stop—numbering over 120 every summer!—has indeed shifted public perceptions of the extraordinary abilities of people with disabilities and of the genuine kindness of fraternity members.

I decided to check out the stop in Denver—named Pedal for Pennies—and when asked to sum up the experience, his first remarks were, "Let me tell you, we had a blast!" The event started out with a bike ride in Denver's City Park neighborhood, which paired each of the area's Special Olympics athletes with one of the cross-country riders. After that, there was a barbecue feast, compelling speakers and, finally, a dance.

I was surprised by just how inclusive the atmosphere was, commenting, "You can be yourself and don't need to impress anybody. Local participants share their joy and positive nature and make everyone feel welcome. Both the riders and the Special Olympic athletes leave feeling encouraged. Both value the human connection that was established."

Pi Kappa Phi riders added to those observations,
describing how the ride left a mark on them:

**"It's just an immense opportunity for personal growth that shows how each
of us can impact each other's lives."** — *Jim from Virginia Tech*

**"My favorite moment was seeing a father cry when his son joined in a limbo dance.
This father had never seen his shy son get involved in a group like this."**
— *Brandon from California State University, Long Beach*

**"My reason for going was to spend time with people with different
abilities. 'Smiles before miles' is the motto, a reminder that, even more
important than the biking, are the connections made at the visits."**
— *Jason from Virginia Tech*

**"Unique and heartwarming, going on the ride has
brought my family closer through fundraising together."**
— *Jack from the University of Colorado Boulder*

"It's amazing to see the difference one person can make."
— *Jared from Virginia Tech*

This journey was undoubtedly life-changing for Bruce Rogers—in more ways than one. As it turns out, it was through the annual ride—through performing an act of kindness—that he met his wife. Five years after his brainstorm, they got married, in 1993. Their three children have also grown up spending every summer involved with the Journey of Hope.

"All of us are better people because of it," Bruce believes.

Some riders take the bike trek only once; many more become lifelong supporters of the nonprofit or other causes that champion kindness. Bruce Rogers has never really left. He still rides for five to seven days with the teams every summer. After staying on The Ability Experience's board of directors for nine years, he now serves on the safety committee for the Journey of Hope, and his firm, Mountaingate Capital, sponsors the ride and the Denver friendship visit.

Summers, when the livin' is hopefully easier for more of us than not, are a good time to consider being part of something that has a mission not unlike that of The Ability Experience—to celebrate kindness and "create a community, one relationship at a time, where the abilities of all people are recognized and valued."

♥

Thank you for the reminder that disability doesn't mean inability, Hanna. Your beautiful story serves as a reminder that volunteering your time and talents is one of the many ways you can channel kindness in your community. To become involved in The Ability Experience, and for ways to volunteer in your community, visit our friends at The Ability Experience.

Lady Gaga

11

KINDNESS AT THE CAT HOUSE

CRYSTAL CHAN

When Lynea Lattanzio first started rescuing cats in central California, she had no plans to become a superhero, let alone the founder of a unique nonprofit organization. But after a couple eye-opening experiences sent her life in an unintended direction, that's pretty much what happened.

When Lynea realized that Fresno County didn't have enough resources to save the many stray cats that were left to fend for themselves, she began to rescue them, and she took care of them in her own home. Just one at first, then another, and then a few more, until she realized there wasn't enough space for her to live alongside the many cats she had rescued. Though she had planned to live a quieter life away from the big city, where she could spend her free time traveling wherever and whenever she wanted, her feline roommates eventually forced her to give up the freedom to come and go as she pleased.

Despite the sacrifices, Lynea never regretted being a mother of adopted cats. The only problem was that there were so many more crying—yes, meowing—for help. That's when she had to tap her own superpowers of imagination, compassion, and kindness. Other skills were important, too. If she had been a veterinarian, her job would have been to treat and save as many animals as possible. If she had been an animal caretaker, her job would have been to feed, groom, bathe, exercise, and care for animals. Once Lynea conceived The Cat House on the Kings—the twelve-acre cat sanctuary and adoption center in Parlier, California, that she founded in the early 1990s—her job had to become a combination of the two.

The sanctuary provides a safe, cage-free, indoor/outdoor residence for abandoned cats and kittens and helps place these rescued animals into loving, permanent homes. The nonprofit also aims to prevent pet overpopulation through a spay and neuter program. In an effort to assist the actual veterinarians the organization employs, Lynea went back to school to train as a veterinary surgical technician.

"I just felt that this was my mission," Lynea acknowledges. "When I started, I didn't realize that it was going to take over all aspects of my life, but I have no regrets."

All the volunteers and workers at The Cat House firmly believe in the mission of the nonprofit. Every employee at The Cat House shares a love of caring for animals, and they are all in the habit of picking up animals found on the side of the road or in alleys and bringing them to the center. Lynea proudly states, "It's like the whole atmosphere of this facility is to take good care of as many animals as we can."

There was one dramatic rescue, for instance, when Armando, the maintenance worker, found an injured cat next to a cemetery on the side of road, with practically only skin and bones left. When Armando found the cat, it was "almost eaten completely by maggots," Lynea recalled.

Saving the cat's life was touch and go, but eventually they succeeded. Everyone working at the center played a role. In honor of the maintenance worker and his act of kindness, it was decided to name the miracle cat "Mando." The road ahead was still challenging. Many months passed before Mando recovered from his injuries, and when he did, Lynea and volunteers at The Cat House were worried he wouldn't find a forever home of his own.

"He was actually kind of wild, so we didn't think he would ever get adopted, but the more love we showed him, the more affectionate he became, and he actually got to the point that he was doing fantastic," Lynea shared. "Now, Mando's the biggest, fattest, most beautiful cat, and he's got a home in Marin."

For Lynea and the rest of The Cat House, helping care for a cat and then watching it fully recover and find a great home is one of the most gratifying experiences. Lynea observed,

"When you do something like that—you take an animal that has nothing left and they fight so hard and you help them—and then they find such a beautiful life, it's very rewarding."

Lynea would love to expand the sanctuary and continue building facilities with special treatment options for animals that are in need for different reasons, whether behavioral or medical—like timid cats, or white cats, who tend to develop skin cancer. This would give them the ability to learn about a variety of issues. Ultimately, Lynea wants to continue improving the lives of as many animals as possible.

An unusual aspect of The Cat House is that its rescued cats are extremely dog-friendly, mainly because the facility also has a number of rescued dogs that live and play with the cats. This may explain why those familiar with The Cat House have nick-named the place "Cat Heaven" and "Dog Disneyland."

At Cat Heaven and Dog Disneyland, volunteers like Terry Noell become the cornerstone of the nonprofit. Terry has been helping out at The Cat House for about fifteen years. He transports adoptees to their new homes, neuters and spays cats, and—as a renaissance man—even deejays at the annual open-house parties that occur twice a year.

Terry began volunteering at The Cat House after his wife, Tammy, asked him for help transporting kittens to their new foster homes. Terry and Tammy then went above and beyond this task by building a special cat room in their house to care for adopted kittens. One of the most moving moments Terry recalls spending at The Cat House was when he buried a cat he rescued, who had died after a fierce battle with feline leukemia.

CRYSTAL CHAN

Terry was so emotionally impacted by the burial, Terry said, that from then on, the memory would let him feel he would "always have a piece of The Cat House with me." The genuine caring and compassion witnessed daily has given him insights into the true meaning of kindness. To Terry, *"kindness is when everyone shows a kind hand and they do everything they can to save every life that passes through the gates."* And that applies to every creature at The Cat House, "regardless of what happens or the conditions or events that led to their arrival."

Lynea echoes Terry's views. To her, "kindness is to feel for the animal, and to understand the pain, fear, and loneliness that the animal is feeling while it's injured."

Everyone at The Cat House may have a different definition of kindness, but having compassion and giving selflessly is definitely at the heart of the nonprofit's mission. Lynea didn't go looking for an opportunity to be kind, yet somehow the opportunity found her.

Everyone knows how I feel about animals, so I too believe that being kind means being kind to all creatures. All any animal wants is to be loved, so thank you, Crystal, for reminding us to be kind to our furry friends. To support Lynea and her mission to rescue animals in the central California area, check out The Cat House on the Kings, and to learn how you can volunteer with a shelter or adopt a rescue animal near you, visit The Humane Society or Best Friends Animal Society.

Lady Gaga

12

The

CHOOSE
LOVE
MOVEMENT

SCARLETT LEWIS

Sometimes things happen in life that we have no control over. This can make us feel powerless. And it's true, things happen that are totally out of our control. But we can take our personal power back when we choose how we respond in any given situation. We always have the choice to thoughtfully respond with love.

I had to put this into practice on December 14, 2012, when the unthinkable happened. My six-year-old son was murdered in his first-grade classroom at Sandy Hook Elementary School alongside nineteen classmates and six educators. It was one of the worst mass murders in US history. In the midst of the powerlessness, horror, and shock we all felt, nothing could change the fact that I could not control the former student who killed all those innocent people. The only way I could take my personal power back would be how I chose to respond to the tragedy. Ultimately, I responded by starting a worldwide movement to choose love through a nonprofit organization I created in honor of my son—the Jesse Lewis Choose Love Movement. Getting there was indeed a process.

Traumatized and beyond comfort at first, I was drawn to the words on our kitchen chalkboard that Jesse must have written the same morning he was killed. Perhaps with spiritual awareness, Jesse, in his best first-grade handwriting, had printed: Nurturing Healing Love. (He spelled them phonetically, as *Norurting Helinn Love*. After all, he was just learning to write.) I knew immediately that if the shooter had been able to give and receive Nurturing Healing Love that the tragedy would never have happened.

We felt comforted by his message and realized it was a prescription for compassion. Despite Jesse's death, those three words reminded me of all that I still had. So I started with gratitude. Despite having lost one of my precious sons, Jesse's older brother, JT, and I still had each other. We live on a small farm with horses, chickens, and dogs that we love. Because of the public nature of our tragedy, it seemed as if the world could feel our pain and everyone wanted to help us heal. We received cards from around the world, most from children, and all from loving people who wished us well. They told us they were holding us in their hearts and praying for us. As our friends and family gathered around us, I felt blessed and loved. We were thankful for the support, and we still are.

Intuitively, I knew that someone who did something so heinous must have been in a tremendous amount of pain. I tried to put myself in his shoes by learning about his life and the suffering he endured. That process helped me to come to a place of forgiveness. When I made the choice to forgive, I remember feeling what seemed like one hundred pounds of anger and resentment lift off my shoulders.

Forgiveness became a key to my ability to heal and be resilient, allowing me to think more clearly, positively, and productively.

I realized it has nothing to do with forgetting, condoning, or being able to hold someone accountable. Forgiveness is simply cutting the cord that attaches you to pain, and suffering, and anger. It is a gift that you give to yourself.

By choosing to focus on being grateful for what I did have and going through the process of forgiveness, I found the strength to step outside my own pain and help others. Instead of focusing internally on my personal situation, I chose to seek answers. I wanted to become part of the solution that could have prevented the tragedy at Sandy Hook Elementary and that would help prevent future tragedies. I found extensive research showing that learning how to have healthy relationships, manage emotions, and be resilient—in other words, social and emotional intelligence—was the number one indicator of a child's future success. I created a program called the Choose Love Enrichment Program that teaches young people everywhere in the world these essential life skills and how to choose love for themselves and others.

The program is free and has steadily gained worldwide momentum as a movement. Choose Love has been an incredible adventure and has shown me how it is possible to heal myself by giving to others and how much we receive when we do champion peace over violence and love over hate. When we help others, we are ultimately helping ourselves. We call this compassion in action.

When the gunman entered Jesse's classroom, his gun jammed. During the short delay, Jesse courageously directed his friends to run, and ultimately saved the lives of nine of his classmates while he remained at his teacher's side, where he died. Jesse left us a powerful formula for choosing love in any situation:

Courage + Gratitude + Forgiveness + Compassion in Action = Choosing Love

When we thoughtfully respond in any situation, circumstance, or interaction by choosing love, we are happier and more resilient; we have better relationships; and we are more likely to make positive and pro social choices.

The Choose Love Movement started at Jesse's funeral when I spoke to those in attendance. It is likely, I shared that day, that the whole tragedy began with an angry thought in the shooter's head. The amazing thing to me is that an angry thought can be changed. I asked everyone that day to consciously change one angry thought into a loving thought each day. This, I offered, is how we become that small pebble of kindness that sends out a ripple effect, creating a safer, more peaceful, and loving world.

Change one thought a day, I repeated, and choose love.

People reported back that just by doing that one simple thing, their lives were changed for the better, forever, and our ripples continue to spread more and more around the globe.

Within us, we have the courage that Jesse showed in his final moments: the courage to be kind; to do what is right; to speak up; and to be our authentic selves. We have the courage to be grateful, even when things are not going our way; the courage to forgive, even when the person who hurt us is not sorry; and the courage to step outside our own pain and help others.

We all have the courage to choose love!

♥

Scarlett, you define bravery and kindness. I had to start and stop reading this story several times. In all of our lives, every day, we are faced with a choice of how to respond to the things happening to us and around us—the mundane and the life changing. To say I am in awe of your commitment to live in a posture of gratitude, compassion, and nurturing and healing love is the understatement of my life, but I thank you. Your movement will save lives, and honor one very, very special one. Please visit the Jesse Lewis Choose Love Movement to join Scarlett's mission to help the world live love a little better, every day.

Lady Gaga

13

THE NINE-YEAR-OLD HERO

HANA MANGAT

There are moments when strangers' lives collide as if by accident, and even though they may never see each other again, they're changed forever. These can be moments when true character is revealed, often through acts of kindness and generosity on the part of unlikely heroes who step forward in the nick of time.

Not long ago, I was a witness to that kind of moment. It was about 1:00 a.m. on one of my last free nights of the summer and, together with my mom and dad, I had just gotten off a very long flight back from the West Coast. Half asleep, my parents and I exited the gate and started to walk through the empty airport toward baggage claim. Out of the corner of my eye, I saw one of our fellow passengers leave the restroom and suddenly fall to the ground.

We immediately ran toward him. My parents, who are doctors by profession, dropped everything and immediately began trying to figure out what had happened. As they asked him questions and searched for a medical information card, the crew from our flight departed the plane and joined our impromptu medical response team.

My parents determined that the man was diabetic and in major need of sugar. As everyone nearby frantically rifled through their luggage for something sweet, the only thing we could seem to find was a protein bar with a minimal amount of chocolate chips. In a barren airport, with security and paramedics taking far too long to respond, we worried that it would not be enough to save him.

Just then, a young boy—named Mecca, as we learned later—arrived at the scene with the flight attendants who had been escorting him to his parents. In the midst of the frantic feeding of the protein bar, Mecca quietly announced: "I have a Snickers in my Lunchables!" No one on the frontlines must have heard him, caught up as they were in the chaos of trying to save a stranger's life, and nobody responded to him. However, Mecca knew what to do. He dug deep into his colorful backpack, opened his snack, and pulled out a Snickers. He then handed it to my father, who was holding the patient on his side while my mother tried to manage with the protein bar.

Within seconds of the Snickers replacing the protein bar, the man regained consciousness, and it was clear to everyone that Mecca, a fourth grader living in Washington, D.C., had saved this stranger's life!

My parents, who have been practicing medicine for almost thirty years, were in awe of the initiative that Mecca took. Afterward my father pointed out, "It was wonderful—very rewarding that a nine-year-old knew what to do and wanted to get involved."

Mecca's mother told us that he has always loved to help people. In fact, Mecca's father would always remind him that his middle name, Naseer, means "helper."

No one could have guessed that earlier that night, Mecca had just been through an ordeal of his own with his flight experience. We came to find out that when Mecca's father's flight was unexpectedly canceled, impromptu accommodations had to be made, forcing Mecca to fly from Oakland, California, to Washington, D.C., alone. He had never flown by himself before and admitted, "I was very nervous about it."

His mother, Kiki Morgain, told us how Mecca's grandmother had filled his backpack with Lunchables to make him a little less anxious. "We worried that he was going to eat all the candy on the flight," Ms. Morgain laughed.

When we told Mecca's parents of his heroic actions, they smiled from ear to ear. Knowing he was nervous about flying alone, they were surprised that he'd saved some candy and were even more surprised that he was able to think about the candy during the emergency he encountered as he got off the plane.

Mecca shrugged, as if to say helping came naturally. "I'm just really, really happy that the man is okay." The next day, he started fourth grade and excitedly told his principal about what had happened. His fourth-grade teacher joked with Mecca, telling him that she sometimes gets low blood sugar and might need Mecca to come to the rescue!

As time goes on, I remain inspired by the experience of witnessing a nine-year-old save a stranger's life, and it still amazes my parents, too. In a very messy, chaotic, and frankly scary world, Mecca's sincerity continues to make us smile.

*My mom put it best:
"To help someone, to be kind
to someone, is a basic human
instinct. In general, people
try to suppress that instinct.
However, it is very evident in
young hearts and should be
encouraged more and more."*

What a helper indeed—way to go, Mecca! I do my best to notice the experiences of the people around me and ask myself if I can help lessen their pain or improve their days. If we could all be a little more like Mecca and pay attention to the people around us and ask, *What do we have that other people might need?* the world would be a better place. Some days, it could be a candy bar that saves the life of a fellow traveler, and other days, it could be a smile to a stranger that has the same effect. Thank you, Hana, your parents, and Mecca for being the helpers.

Lady Gaga

LEARNING TO HEAL

14

KIRAH HORNE

A BROKEN HEART

A *miracle.*

As far back as I can remember, that was the word my parents used to describe me. And, at least until the second grade, I believed them.

I can remember looking at myself in the mirror as a little girl and, instead of being self-conscious about the raised scar that spreads over most of my chest—from just above my ribs up to my collarbone—I felt lucky.

The scar was a daily reminder of the open-heart surgery I underwent as a five-year-old to correct a rare birth defect—and proof of the miracle that the problem was detected before it was too late. My parents were told that if the doctor hadn't heard my heart murmur, then by the time I turned twelve I would have literally dropped dead one day in the middle of playing volleyball—or something like it—and no one would have known why.

My parents pointed out that part of the miracle of my situation had to do with the fact that I was a shy kid who didn't talk a lot. So it was normal at the doctor's office for me to be quiet—one factor that may have made it easier for him to hear the murmur.

Back then, of course, I didn't understand the severity of my condition and what wound up being two surgeries in one day. The first operation was to correct the defect, and the second was to remove a needle that had been left in my heart by accident. Like most kids, my focus was on getting out of the hospital as soon as possible and returning to my friends at preschool. My parents never said that I could have died, only that I had come through the ordeal with flying colors.

The feeling I had of being lucky, or special even (but in a good way), stayed with me for the next couple of years. The scar, sometimes reddish and angry-looking, other times a ghostly white, was something I grew used to wearing as a badge of honor. Even if I didn't show it to many people, my scar was no big deal—just a part of me that I couldn't think to see as something negative.

But not everyone saw the miracle.

In second grade, after making a new close friend that year, I felt comfortable enough with her to talk about my life-saving surgery at age five. "See?" I said, pointing out one of the top branches of the scar that could be seen over the collar of my shirt.

"*Ewwwww!*" she shrieked. "Get away from me! You're sick!"

Looking back, I don't blame her for what she said. She reacted as many children might. But the hurt was tough to erase. Worse was that, all of a sudden, I became increasingly self-conscious about my scar.

From then on, I didn't want anyone to see it ever again.

For months, even years, I kept playing the words "You're sick!" over and over again in my head. The miracle—the one thing that had saved my life—was now a source of shame.

As I got into middle school, kids stopped bullying me about my heart surgery scar and moved on to other things. They'd point out my quirks, mocking me for being gullible and naive—and for seeking refuge in the music of Lady Gaga, a role model and an inspiration to me, whose profound lyrics helped me through some terribly dark times.

Much to my shock, in the eighth grade, my musical taste and choice of role models earned the disdain of my favorite teacher, who didn't think my views lived up to his standards. When he called me "Freak" in front of the entire class, I could barely breathe.

The power of those words hit me harder than I could measure. They were words, unfortunately, that I, as an eight-year-old, took deeply to heart. Though I had no words yet to describe her treatment of me, this was the first of many times I would be bullied over the next several years.

What? He. Just. Called. Me. A. F-F-F-FREEEEAKKK? Why? Why?

This offhand slam was from an adult, in front of all my peers. This was in a place where I was supposed to feel safe. Now I couldn't even escape the harsh words of a teacher—no longer my favorite—who had made me feel very much unsafe.

> *"Freak" cut me to the core, like a sword going through my body, slicing me even more because it came from an adult who we all thought was cool, in front of all my classmates.* **What will they think of me now?** *The question burned in my mind, adding fuel to the fire of anxiety already burning inside.*

A turbulent period followed.

After that incident, I began having daily panic attacks, most acute when I was in that class. The panic episodes were emotionally draining, and I felt emptier after every single one of them. Soon I began to build up the emotional scar tissue of just not caring about anything. Before long, the attacks began to hurt my grades. Never had I failed a class before, but I ended up with an *F* in algebra that year and had to retake it as a freshman in high school. Instead of recognizing that I was suffering from an anxiety disorder, I assumed this meant I wasn't intelligent.

In my downward spiral, I was harder on myself than anyone else could have been, calling myself names inside my head, which stressed me out so much, I was constantly sick. Over the next three years, I lost many close friends. It wasn't that they didn't care, but in reality, they had their own problems and didn't need mine on top of theirs.

The pressure in my chest became constant. The feeling of suffocation was all-consuming. Before I hit rock bottom, I tried to pull myself up. Nothing made me feel better. At one point, I stopped eating. That was probably the lowest point in my life. As much as I wanted to give up, I never did.

Whenever anyone asked, "Hey, are you okay?" I'd shrug and say, "I'm fine!"

Maybe I was good at faking it. Many people who know me pretty well still don't know how low I sank. My reason for keeping everything inside was that I didn't want anyone to see me as weak or incapable of pulling myself together. The irony is that by doing so, I denied myself the help I desperately needed.

Today I know that there are lots of resources available for people who struggle with anxiety, depression, and similar issues (or ones that are even worse). Let me just add, dear reader, that if you're struggling in silence, I encourage you to seek out those resources. Help really *is* available!

Sadly, in those days I somehow didn't know that I could even ask for help. Most of the time I was so busy feeling worthless that it felt as though I were drowning. At fourteen, I felt myself crashing into a complete mental breakdown. All I wanted was for it to end.

How could I ever reach out to anyone for help when it seemed the entire world was against me?

Instead of forcing myself to find help, one day in the cafeteria, when I was in the ninth grade and was being bullied, help found me.

That moment of kindness—from someone I barely knew—saved my life.

Minutes earlier, as I walked around looking for a place to sit—feeling the familiar pressure in my heart telling me I could no longer join the group of friends who had decided to cast me out, trying to tune out mean looks and comments that told me I wasn't welcome—I could not have felt more alone. But lo and behold, the next thing I knew this friendly girl waved me over to where she was sitting, basically taking me in and letting me eat lunch with her.

Suddenly, I didn't have to be alone anymore. To this day, she and I still eat lunch together. Life, slowly but surely, began to improve.

By the end of my high school sophomore year, there were other friends who'd taken me under their wings, too, who have been there for me ever since. Instead of mocking me for the music and media I love, my friends embrace me for being who I am—quirks and all—and for my love of artists whose lyrics remind me of myself. This included Gaga, of course, but also Sia, Lana Del Rey, and Eminem. Now I can talk about the shows I watch—like *Bones*, *New Girl*, and *Grey's Anatomy*—whose characters are quirky, like me, as they go through their trials and tribulations and make it through successfully.

Through my own trials, I learned that I'm stronger than I could ever have once believed and that, even with everything I've been through, it was possible to make myself whole again. The toughest lesson was learning that I could ask for help when needed and that I shouldn't be afraid to do so.

A little kindness from someone else goes a long way. So much so that, in turn, I learned that I could take all of this pain that had the power to make me feel so broken and put it toward something more positive. True! When I signed up to volunteer at the local humane society, I was amazed at how much stress could be relieved by taking care of living beings who can't take care of themselves and need just as much help, if not more, than I do.

No longer do I feel ashamed of my surgery or any parts of my story, no matter how embarrassing or painful. Not that I want to walk around with my scar on my sleeve. But if one person can relate and my talking about it helps them, even a little bit, the pain won't be in vain.

Yes, words do have power over our lives. To anyone struggling, my words are simple:

Thank you, Kirah, for being honest about your struggles and showing strength in the face of adversity. We cannot let other people define us with their negative words. No matter what anyone says, remember that you are strong, brave, and beautiful. If you or someone you know is experiencing bullying, please reach out to an adult you trust and tell them how you're feeling. For more resources on bullying, check out STOMP Out Bullying or The Cybersmile Foundation.

Lady Gaga

You don't have to suffer alone.

Find a teacher, a friend, or a guardian you can trust and tell them how you feel. Remember, no one will know unless you say something. Most people don't wish you any harm, and telling them how you feel takes so much of the weight off your shoulders. We are not weak just because our emotions take hold of us sometimes. Strength comes in numbers.

A miracle is not like someone waving a magic wand and making everything in your life perfect. Believe me, I still struggle with letting my scar show, and I do still have panic attacks and bouts of really dark depression. But whenever I feel even the slightest twitch of darkness returning, I try to put my focus on something more positive—maybe by helping someone else going through a hard time. No, nothing is perfect, and I may not be 100 percent all the time yet, but I don't let the invisible needles left in my heart get the best of me.

The miracle is that I really do have a healthy and loving heart, I have what it takes to overcome the bad days, and I've got a million reasons to know I can.

15

THE GIFT OF ASKING FOR HELP

ROSE NGUYEN

In my memory, there's a dividing line between my old-fashioned, happy life up until early in the ninth grade and everything else that followed. Before high school, the world I recall was a warm and welcoming place for me and my family—my dad, mom, and younger brother. My father was our anchor: wise, and a very handy man. He knew answers to what seemed like every question I ever had. In our traditional Vietnamese, hardworking immigrant household, he led the way, and the future seemed defined, certain, and solid.

Naively, I suppose, before entering high school, I expected the next four years to somehow play out much like a teen movie, à la Disney's *High School Musical*: an adorable love story filled with singing and dancing on tables and (as long as I kept up my grades) lots of free time for socializing. My fantasy could not have been more wrong.

In October 2015, with no warning signs, my father suddenly passed away from a ruptured aneurysm in his brain. His departure left behind an open wound—a wound that still has not fully healed.

With the loss of my father, overnight the world went from a safe place to a foreign and foreboding land. When I began experiencing many "firsts" without him—my first time flying on a plane alone, my first time driving alone, my first time facing heartbreak, my first time questioning my own existence—I couldn't help but yearn for his presence.

Initially, after this unexpected tragedy, I managed to resume my daily life, acting as much as possible like everything was normal—partly by conditioning myself not to validate my grief. Mainly, because I was young, I just didn't know how to handle the painful loss of a loved one. And so, despite raw feelings of shock and confusion that I held within, I opted to take on the responsibility of being the English-speaking representative for my mom and a caregiver to my younger brother. Those roles gave me cover so that I could mask the unfamiliar pain below the surface. Slowly, I got through the school year.

Once summer came around, however, I lost hope that the lingering cloud above my head would go away, as it was now not only lingering but raining above my head. The submerged emotions I'd spent ninth grade doing a good job of hiding from others became unmanageable. Almost inevitably, I lost my commonsense grip on reality. Inside I'd be asking, *How could this be happening to me?*

Why can't I find my way back to solid ground?

No voices would answer. And I was convinced there was no one who could help me with my burdens. Being raised in my very private, traditional Vietnamese household—where personal emotions were not addressed either because of

language barriers or cultural differences—I was unable to talk openly to my mom or other family members about my father's death.

Without anywhere to turn, I felt stuck.

Soon, I fell into my biggest slump. Daily routines became harder to carry out. Getting out of bed every morning felt like an internal war with no actual winner, attending school was no longer enjoyable, and living no longer felt . . . real.

ROSE NGUYEN

Even as my feelings of despair and disorientation intensified, I refused to confide in anyone. The people who believed in my tough persona—I'd be letting them down if I told them about my irrational thoughts. It was too awkward to bring up my father's death in any situation. The last thing I wanted was pity. My way of coping, then, was to continue bottling up all the negative energy by focusing on my academics and my family's well-being. The cycle seemed endless: go to school, complete extracurriculars, work on house chores, translate documents, babysit my brother.

The naive girl I once was—the girl who thought her life was going to resemble *High School Musical*—could never have imagined she'd succumb to a period of self-harming. It began to happen, though. Because I couldn't allow myself to show vulnerability at home, self-harm felt like the only way to experience a tangible, physical pain and still divert the unfamiliar emotions. This was the lowest depth of my darkest time. Looking back, it's clear I was simply desperate to find release from my suffocating cloud by reaching for another outlet of pain.

Ironically, during this phase, I continued to attend school, laugh with friends, and bond with my mother and brother, as though I had put the tragedy behind me. Finally I reached a turning point as the first few months of junior year passed and the physical pain of self-harming no longer had any real effect. The voice in my head was still there, but now it was egging me on:

Who says you have to do this all on your own?

Why can't you just ask for help?

The time had come for me to do just that and confide in my closest friends.

Taking those first steps—daring to ask friends if I could talk to them about my mental state—was the most relieving yet terrifying feeling all at once. The terror came from worry about what would happen if I let down my guard. The relief came from my friends' utmost generosity of heart. When I opened up about my struggles, I was greeted with respect, acknowledgment, and advice. They surrounded me with a huge amount of love and support that I will be eternally thankful for. They even made me feel that I was honoring them with the gift of my trust. Bit by bit, I steered away from self-harming and, at long last, faced the reality of my own state of grief.

Many of us never let ourselves acknowledge the pain of our losses. When we don't, I've learned, it's that much harder to heal. Some of us also dive into caring for others but deny ourselves the emotional care we need and deserve, too. One reason I didn't talk to my friends about my father dying was because I understood that none of them could really relate. Yet there's nothing wrong with explaining to someone else how it feels to go through something they haven't. When I began to talk to them and to give voice to my own feelings, it was painful but so liberating. The best way to describe it, I found, was that, **at the time, losing my dad was like a tree losing all its rusty leaves once winter came, leaving me to feel lonely and abandoned**.

♥

I am extremely proud of Rose for sharing how she felt after losing her father and reaching out for help when she was engaging in self-harm. I've been open about my own journey and I, too, learned that loving and respecting yourself — your mind and your body — are important ways to ensure you are healthy. If you are struggling with self-harm, visit To Write Love on Her Arms, or for more information as to how you can get help, check out Project Semicolon.

Lady Gaga

Today I am still in the process of healing, but I now feel a sense of peace with my grief after accepting it's possible to learn to heal from sorrow. After three years, I made it a goal to be patient with myself and trust the process of life and growth to see me through.

With all that I have learned, three important lessons about loss stand out:

1. *BE PATIENT WITH YOURSELF.* If you've lost a loved one, it's okay to be angry, sad, lost, and any other emotions that come up. Feelings are completely valid. We each have a different time clock when it comes to processing grief, so don't force yourself to adhere to someone else's schedule. Be kind to yourself. Let those around you know if you are ready to talk or not; you can guide them through your journey of healing as well. Soon enough, the pain you are feeling will slowly become more bearable. Trust the process. There is kindness in this world for you, too.

2. *ALWAYS REMEMBER THE GOOD THINGS ABOUT YOUR LOVED ONE.* So many times I've heard a song or smelled a certain scent that reminds me of my dad. Hold on to loving memories. Let yourself laugh at funny moments shared in the past or cry at the sadder memories. Cherish the gift of those memories and share them with others. It's a way of keeping the spirit of your loved one alive.

3. *BE GRATEFUL FOR THE TIME YOU HAD WITH YOUR LOVED ONE.* Be grateful not only for the people you've had in your life but also for the times when they helped you to grow and improve yourself. Avoid feeling like the world owes you something—a feeling of entitlement diminishes who you are. No matter how rough going your grieving period is, trust that, in time, their memory will pave the way toward healing and all will be well.

The more time goes by, the more I find new ways to connect to my dad's memory. High school was not exactly the musical I'd once dreamed, but it has not been without joy and growth. My father would be proud to know that I'm resourceful and resilient, and that I believe I am truly capable of anything I put my heart and mind toward. Even if I don't know how it's all going to shake out, I know that the future doesn't have to be faced alone.

No, I'm not Superwoman, and sometimes I battle self-doubt, but I am okay with not being okay all the time. There will continue to be many firsts, seconds, and thirds without my father beside me physically. But as long as I choose, he will always be close to my heart, living in my memories. My traumatic circumstances do not define my life, but instead empower me to reach for bigger and brighter stars.

16

MEMORIES CAN SOMETIMES BE THE BEST MEDICINE

NICHOLAS McCARDLE

You never know when, where, or how an act of kindness will arrive at a moment when you most need it—but if you open yourself to that possibility, you may be surprised by how quickly it can make every difference in the world.

For Kensey Bergdorf, unprecedented loss struck her existence not long after she finished her freshman year at West Virginia University, where she was studying multidisciplinary studies as well as immunology and medical microbiology. At the age of nineteen, having never faced the loss of a loved one, Kensey's father died suddenly, followed two days later by the death of her grandmother. In the immediate aftermath, Kensey recalls, "It was earth-shattering. You grow up instantly."

Lost and unsure how to even begin to cope, welcomed wisdom showed up right away when a friend offered her advice after the funerals, saying: "You need to write down everything you can remember about them, because memories don't last forever, and you're going to want those. You're going to want those little reminders, because ten years from now you may not remember these things."

Kensey hurriedly started jotting down all the memories of her loved ones she could remember. From trips to the zoo with her dad to the distinct smell of woodsmoke at her grandmother's house, she captured it all within the lined sheets of a notebook. Pages upon pages of her thoughts and memories were compiled. Every day she could visit her loved ones in stories she might have otherwise forgotten, almost like collecting treasures for a chest to be opened some time in the future. The process of writing was also cathartic and empowering. The point was to pour out all her thoughts and feelings. Things that she couldn't talk about were easy to let flow onto paper. The notebook wasn't going to judge her. On the contrary, it allowed her to "get out of my funk."

Five months after the deaths of her father and grandmother, Kensey's best friend suddenly lost her dad. Grateful for the kind advice that had been given to her, Kensey brought the family notebooks so that they could all start journaling their memories together. After additionally losing two friends, Kensey had an idea for a project that would elevate the power of journaling for grief and loss to a more structured level—and let her help more of her fellow students. When she approached the university's Department of Leadership Studies for funding to get a project launched, however, nothing much happened.

Then, in an unplanned moment at a scholarship dinner, she found herself seated next to Dr. Lisa Di Bartolomeo, a world language professor at West Virginia University, and somehow the conversation led to Kensey's interest in starting the Memory Journal Project.

"It was such a striking idea that I told her immediately, 'I want to help,'" says Dr. Di Bartolomeo. "I saw how inspired she was by the thought of helping others work through their losses. It was wonderful to see someone take their own pain and reach out to help others work through theirs, and I was just floored by Kensey's ability to channel that loss into action."

Kensey was then able to work with individuals from the office of student life and the Carruth Center—the mental health clinic on campus—to start drafting a guideline for students to record their memories. The goal at hand was to create therapeutic prompts and activities to engage those who were using it, and Kensey accomplished just that. After getting the guideline polished up and the notebooks finished, they were made available to everyone on campus.

♥

Dealing with grief is never easy; thank you, Nicholas, for highlighting a healthy way to cope with loss in Kensey's memory books. There is a beautiful quote by one of my favorite writers, Rainer Maria Rilke, that says, "Let everything happen to you, beauty and terror. Just keep going, no feeling is final." I've found peace in those words, and I hope you do, too. Remember, if you're hurting, you're not alone, so please consider creating your own memory book, joining a support group, or talking through your feelings. For more resources on how to do this, check out The Dougy Center or the National Alliance for Grieving Children.

Lady Gaga

Kim Mosby, senior associate dean of students, describes how Kensey galvanized attention, not just to the issues of loss and grief but to the potential of finding a positive outlet and a support group. Mosby says, "She was very focused and determined to bring this to our campus, and we all got behind her in this endeavor."

Kensey explains that helping other people find an outlet for their grief "is everything to me. It was so horrible for me, and I don't want anyone else to go through that." She wanted to offer more than the generic grief pamphlets that are often handed out. She wanted her *Memory Journal Guide Book* to feel as encouraging as the advice first given to her when she was grappling with the over-whelming anger that she had to get off her chest. So she included prompts for writing and drawing, along with suggested activities for retrieving memories. Her hope was to give others the same permission she was given to turn her journaling into a "brain dump," as she calls it.

Kensey's *Memory Journal Guide Book* has already spread beyond her college and local communities as a therapeutic tool for anyone going through the grieving process. The healing properties of writing and focusing on memories of loved ones are well known in therapy settings, but what makes Kensey's method unique is that it is written from the point of view of someone who has gone through the emotional roller coaster of loss and come out the other side. Kensey has even adapted a version of the guide for younger children to use when they lose someone they love and want to remember.

"I took a kind thing that someone did for me and amplified it," Kensey points out. "I encourage people to take the things that they appreciate and then try to emulate those in their own lives."

At some time in all of our lives, loss does become inevitable. When that time comes, hopefully you will gain guidance from the kind, loving advice once given to Kensey, which she has continued to pass on to others. Her example is a wonderful reminder of how kindness can heal, transform, and inspire. Kensey, who graduated from WVU with two degrees and is pursuing her PhD at Vanderbilt University in pharmacology, is quick to note that it's never too late to start your own memory journal. For just a few bucks, you can pick up some notebooks and pen or pencil for yourself (or a friend) and begin journaling your memories today.

You'll be creating a treasure chest that's yours to keep forever.

17

POETIC FORMS OF ENGAGEMENT

TAYLOR M. PARKER

Ashley Dun and Jesse Cale—founding partners of the Columbus, Ohio–based Secret Midnight Press—have a fascinating story to tell. And they believe it is through our most deeply felt stories that we dare to tell to others that bonds of kindness, compassion, and connection are forged.

Their success has been self-made. As they describe on their company's website (in a chapter they've titled "Friends That Cry Together, Ride Together"), in their younger days they were the kind of friends who would huddle together to talk about "the saddest songs they've ever heard and favorite films specifically ending in tragedy." Once adulthood hit, the friendship continued, and eventually they decided to "finish the books they had always talked about writing." But why stop at creating poetry, stories, music, and more? Why not launch a "publishing company and curiosity brand"?

In a short amount of time, the two accomplished that ambitious goal and more—publishing poetry collections individually and together. Rather than waiting to be given a publishing deal, or looking for an outside venue to offer them a safe space for their authentic voices to be heard or a music platform for performance opportunities, Dun and Cale had the courage to basically hire themselves by creating those outlets on their own. They soon went on to expand their team and are now growing a stable of authors while building an impressive international audience and a global community of fellow creatives. As the two perform and travel the country, as well as Europe, their shows include invitations for audience members to "share their art and share their heart," through an open-mic platform.

Definitely a dynamic duo, Dun and Cale generously empower their followers to embrace their own truths, gifts, and the creative voices that set them apart—just as the two of them have.

Cale, a poet and musician, refers to himself as a "deep-feeling, magic being" and has said that he wants to be known as "a storyteller, an imaginative person, and a creator." Raised on bedtime stories his father used to make up on the spot, Cale has a lot to say about how stories forge connections between the teller and the listener:

> **"I've lived a very interesting life, and I love recalling it to tell stories . . . how people describe things—like the taste of food or the way they felt after watching a movie or hearing a certain song—is even storytelling . . . Everything can be a story. It's all about how people fall in love with life, the things that they love in life, and the things that make you hurt that people like to talk about. When it comes down to it, it's the things that make you *feel* that you talk about and that can become the story."**

Dun, who has called herself a "highly sensitive person and empath," has spoken about how sharing stories can be a means of offering kindness and helping to promote empathy—whether for oneself or for others:

> **"Being kind and empathetic makes my life easier—because if somebody does something that hurts me, I'm able to be sensitive to their story and how their brokenness may have led them to that. It helps me not hold on to bitterness and have the fulfillment of deep relationships in these times. It's interesting, as a woman, to be accepted as sensitive, and it can be perceived as weak (which I do not want), but I go on stage every night to share my art. I just hope that it can inspire more women and more people to be sensitive and authentic."**

Audience members who have attended their events around the nation are evidence of the impact that the work of Secret Midnight Press has already achieved. Event attendees echo the fact that these performances not only establish and sustain a community for creatives but also inspire others to join in sharing their stories, being kind to themselves, and finding strength in vulnerability—a key ingredient in self-expression and art.

The Secret Midnight Press events, said one fan, made them feel "safe and supported" and seemed to make strangers feel as if they're surrounded by friends. Another attending poet said, "I couldn't feel alone here, no matter what I'm going through."

Others who have been part of the events—both in this country and abroad—express deep gratitude to the two inspiring poets for creating a platform where all are encouraged to share stories, poetry, music, and other creative efforts. To those seeking input about how to go further as creatives, and to all young or aspiring poets and storytellers, Ashley Dun and Jesse Cale have special messages for you:

"Have grace always. Stay rooted in love and compassion for others and for yourself. Be brave. Speak up and speak out. Ask for help when you need it. Know that things will be okay."
—ASHLEY DUN

"Share your heart. Don't be so hard on yourself. Please try to be a friend to yourself, no matter how hard that may be."
—JESSE CALE

If you can't make it to a Secret Midnight Press event anytime soon, why not create a similar type of event at a welcoming place near you? It may be one of the kindest things you could do for yourself or for someone else.

Singing, songwriting, and dancing are powerful forms of expression, so I'm thrilled Taylor highlighted how important expressing yourself can be and how we don't need an invitation, a record deal, a publishing offer, etc., to share our experiences in the world. In whatever form you choose to do this in, we're proud of you for bravely sharing your feelings with someone. If you don't know where to start, check out Power Poetry, the world's first and largest mobile poetry community for youth, and be sure to check out Channel Kindness to read more stories about expressing yourself kindly.

Lady Gaga

18

HELPING TRANS-GENDER YOUTH

MARIA MONGIARDO

From Boston, Massachusetts, Cameron Russo—who is in his early twenties—could write a textbook on courage, compassion, and kindness. With bravery and optimism, he shares an overview of a huge portion of his life in his YouTube video "My Female to Male Transgender Story"—which has been viewed close to seven hundred thousand times.

Telling his full story wasn't easy, but Cameron knew it was important for many reasons. For starters, he wanted to bring awareness from his personal experience as to what it means to be trans. Simply stated, *transgender* is a term for people whose gender identity, expression, and/or behavior is different from those typically associated with their assigned sex at birth.

Early in his journey, Cameron decided to chronicle aspects of his life through various social media outlets. He recalls, "I started using social media to document my photos and thoughts while I was transitioning."

When his content began to get some attention, he realized that, with this platform, the act of opening up would allow him to educate and expose more people to who transgender individuals are. He knew that really putting himself out there with YouTube might draw unwanted attention, but he'd also never forgotten what it was like to go through all the stages of transition without guidance.

Cameron acknowledges, "I was alone throughout my whole transition, hormones, and surgery, so having someone there, even over the Internet, is a huge help." The opportunity to be kind, even if it meant telling difficult parts of his journey, was something he couldn't ignore. He was strongly motivated to put his story out there in an even more public way for one major reason: "Because life's too short, as cliché as that is. I spent so much time hating myself, and now I wish I could get those years back. I see so many people struggling, and I just want to help them."

In addition to regularly making videos on YouTube and offering advice to trans youth while talking, as he says, to both "pre-transitioned guys and those who are just starting out, to help them find more comfort," Cameron now inspires countless members of the LGBTQ+ community.

I was fortunate, as a youth reporter for Channel Kindness, to interview Cameron about his story so far. In his most widely viewed YouTube video, he goes back to a moment in 2006 when, at age nine, his parents were divorced and he moved to a new school—and began to feel a disconnect. As high school approached, a feeling of certainty developed about wanting to be a boy.

CHANNEL KINDNESS: When did you know you were trans?

CAMERON: I came out as trans when I was fourteen years old but discovered the term at age thirteen. Once I found out what it was, it just clicked.

The transition from female to male was met with criticism and rejection, including what happened when Cameron's mother listened to the statement, "I want to cut my hair and be a guy," and then said, "I know you better than you know yourself, and you are a girl." That had hurt a great deal because of the painful effort it had taken to come out in the first place. His stepfather was even more critical, blaming Cameron for the tension in the household—which led Cameron to multiple suicide attempts. Through the help of a therapist and Cameron's own efforts—he worked nonstop to earn the money required for hormonal therapy and surgery—upon high school graduation, he successfully made his transition. He has an excellent relationship with his mom now and with his biological father, both of whom are very supportive and loving, though he remains estranged from his stepdad.

After all of that, are his painful days behind him?

CAMERON: I am a lot happier now. This time it is genuine happiness.

CHANNEL KINDNESS: What advice do you have for other trans youth?

CAMERON: Hang in there. Life may seem like it is at a standstill right now, and you feel like you are never going to get to where you want to be, but I promise you will get there. Be proud of who you are.

CHANNEL KINDNESS: What got you into making YouTube videos?

CAMERON: I started making videos on YouTube because, on Tumblr, a follower of mine asked me to do a question-and-answer, so I made a video and put it on YouTube. Once I started doing that, I started to really enjoy it, so I made more. I just got a new camera for my videos instead of having to use my Mac to record. My videos are on a lot of transgender-related topics, like top surgery and testosterone. I also make "story time" videos about random things that have happened in my life.

CHANNEL KINDNESS: What do you hope people understand from reading about you and your story?

CAMERON: For the first year of my transition, I was stealth outside of the Internet, meaning I was not open about being transgender. I always felt people would be weirded out by me, because I saw so many people bash on trans people online. When people read my story, I just want them to understand that just because I changed my gender does not make me crazy or "sick in the head" like I have been told. I was not happy, and I was on the road to ending my life, so I had to change what I knew was wrong. I want people to watch my videos and realize that things can get so much better once you put yourself first.

CHANNEL KINDNESS: What has surprised you most about sharing your story?

CAMERON: When I told my whole story from beginning to end in a video recently, that was the first time I ever spoke about it out loud. Just initially, it reached over four hundred thousand people and was briefly in a Diane Sawyer *20/20* special on ABC. The amount of people who messaged me after that video was mind-blowing. It was crazy to see how similar other people's stories were—they were just too scared to be open about it. But because I was, they opened up to me.

Cameron's courage has earned him well-deserved applause from many in the LGBTQ+ community and from allies who may not be part of the community but want to help. Knowing that a disproportionately high percentage of gay, lesbian, bisexual, and transgender people have attempted suicide, Cameron hopes to encourage everyone to consider looking for ways to help and support the LGBTQ+ community. He recommends, "Every summer, there is a Pride parade in almost every state. It is really fun, and so many people go. Even if you do not fall in the L, G, B, T, or Q+, it is always better with more people. Educating others is so important. Since social media is so big nowadays, sharing videos is so easy, and it reaches a lot of people. A really simple way of being involved in the community is just by being kind."

YOU DESERVE

SAFETY · HOME · LOVE

♥ ☆ 🎄 ☆ ♥

.... · ... *stay strong*

♥

I love Cameron's wise advice and am so grateful to you, Maria, for sharing it. Life is too short to spend any time hating yourself, so if you're lucky enough to be able to embrace yourself and who you are, we encourage you to share your story and help other people accept themselves as well. Thank you for your bravery, Cameron. We're so glad you're here. If you or someone you know needs more resources to support their transition journey, please visit Trans Lifeline, Human Rights Campaign, or the Lambda Legal Defense and Education Fund.

Lady Gaga

Cameron Russo is the definition of someone who has chosen to channel kindness, adding in equal parts courage and compassion, and I predict he will continue to grow in his role as a leader of a movement of inclusion, acceptance, and empowerment.

19

IT TAKES A WHILE TO Learn TO BE Human

ISAIAH MORGAN

When you become a channel for kindness, both for the giving and the receiving of it, you learn that you are never really alone as long as you're able to take the first steps to ask for help . . . OR to offer it. At a community health center based in Southern Colorado, Josh—a peer specialist who works in the organization's recovery solutions area—knows that truth well.

For a long time the stigma associated with mental illness kept Josh from talking about his own struggles with anxiety and depression. That is until he suffered a breakdown on the job and desperately sought help. Josh remembers that the day it happened, when he first met a peer specialist, was the moment that saved his life.

Not only was he given tools and resources to understand and cope with his own issues, but also, along the way, found his own calling to help others who struggle with mental illness.

Peer specialists like Josh can be all the more effective because they've been on the receiving end of the help. After starting as someone who needed and used Health Solutions' mental health services, it wasn't long before Josh recognized that helping others in the same fashion was exactly the kind of career he wanted to pursue.

At Recovery Solutions—which Josh calls "a place where people [with mental illness] can go to fit in"—he has gained a lot of expertise since 2016, when he first came on board as a peer specialist. However, just as important as the training and knowledge you can attain, he believes, is the life experience you offer. After all, as Josh points out, you can claim to fully understand mental illness, but you can't really understand it unless you've lived it.

Although he has never thought of himself as brave, by speaking openly and honestly about his mental health story Josh exemplifies true courage. And so without even knowing it, he seems to have mastered the art of bravery—a quality that allows others to feel safe in his presence.

Even if it's not easy to be public about his issues with anxiety and depression, he sees the positive impact that doing so has had on the community. He's able to show that someone with mental illness, even with noticeable symptoms, can still have a steady job, car, and house. More than that, he wants to continue to show that it's possible to be someone known to have had mental illness and still contribute to society and lead a fulfilling, happy life.

When asked what convinced him to get treatment after his breakdown, Josh admits he was inspired by the example of strangers. Some were fictional characters accepting help within storylines from movies and television; others were famous actors who publicly worked through their own mental health challenges. There was tough-guy mob boss Tony Soprano on the HBO series *The Sopranos*—spoiler alert!—who dealt with debilitating panic attacks. These attacks landed him in therapy early in season one, and the sessions continued for the rest of the series. Josh also knew that Carrie Fisher (the late actress who depicted Princess Leia in the *Star Wars* movies) dealt openly with her bipolar disease. Media and culture clearly helped, in Josh's view, to destigmatize mental illness and certainly prodded him to get needed help.

For anyone reading this story who wants to channel kindness for someone suffering from mental illness, you could actually become the first point of outreach in their support system. Josh has identified what he considers to be the three most important phrases in the mental health field, and he has told himself these same phrases before.

They are:

"Let me know how I can support you."

"I believe you."

"It's real, but you will get through this."

Those phrases can also be used in everyday conversations with friends, family members, or coworkers who just need a sounding board. They summon kindness, which Josh defines beautifully by saying,

"Kindness is an interaction where everyone involved leaves feeling better than they did before."

Empathy is crucial to being kind, Josh believes, just as he thinks being kind is a key to personal happiness.

What else can we do to help others in crisis? As a society, he would love to see us all do more to be kind to one another by embracing a culture that prioritizes mental health and advocates for those in need—instead of stigmatizing anyone with an issue. At the very least, as a society, we can ask people struggling with their mental health, "How can I support you?"

We can listen and learn more from one another. Josh said it best: "It takes a while to learn how to be human."

Inspired by Josh to look for ways you can become a kinder, braver, more empathetic person? Then he's got some good advice for you: "Forget the Golden Rule, or the Platinum Rule. Treat others how *they* want to be treated."

Isaiah, you start your piece so powerfully, I just need to repeat it again: *When you become a channel for kindness, both for the giving and the receiving of it, you learn that you are never really alone.* You are so right. One of the kindest things we can do is to be honest with ourselves and authentically share our story. What you may find by telling your story is that in doing so, it validates your emotions and makes it easier for other people to tell their stories. People are more likely to feel safer, more comfortable, and less alone when they hear about someone who has gone through a similar experience. To share your story and read about other people's stories, we encourage you to check out StoryCorps or The Moth.

Lady Gaga

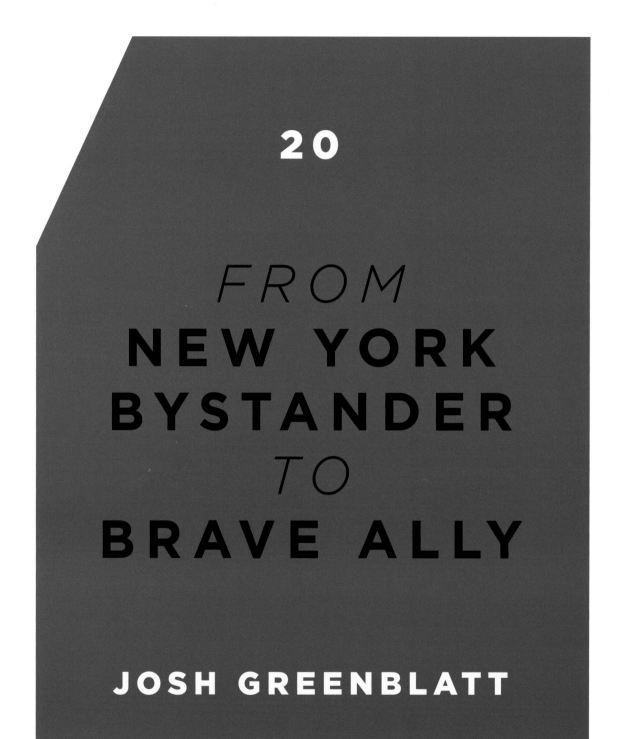

20

FROM
NEW YORK
BYSTANDER
TO
BRAVE ALLY

JOSH GREENBLATT

Courage can be hard to call on when hate shows its face.

In my memories, I can still see images of that face and hear its voice. I can remember a woman yelling at me, warning that when I got off the subway, her friends would beat me up. I remember a man whispering in my ear that he had just gotten out of prison, that he had murdered people, and that he really needed my money. I remember walking, minding my own business, when someone started hurling all sorts of slurs and insults at me. The list of moments when I have felt unsafe, frozen in panic, goes on and on.

But there's another list of mine that is even longer and haunts me even more. It's the list of moments when I have seen someone else's safety being threatened and did not intervene.

I'm ashamed to admit it, but the same fear that paralyzed me when I was being targeted always seemed to overtake me when I saw someone else being harassed. That's why, when I saw it, I instantly clicked the article on a friend's social media post about bystander intervention training.

The article noted that in the wake of the 2016 election, there was a steep rise in the number of Islamophobia-related incidents. A young New York–based woman who happens to be Muslim and wears a hijab no longer felt comfortable walking home by herself. Her friends put out a request on Facebook for people who would be willing to walk with her. And it went viral. More than three thousand everyday New Yorkers immediately signed the Google Doc—with another five thousand signing soon afterward.

Practically overnight, the overwhelming response from total strangers led to the creation of The Accompany Project. An initiative of the Arab American Association of New York (AAANY), The Accompany Project's goal, as they describe it, is "to train thousands of New Yorkers to disrupt violence—particularly against Arab, Muslim, and undocumented residents—and to organize for stronger, safer neighborhoods." And it all began with a simple, brave gesture of concern to help one young woman who felt unsafe.

The Accompany Project's volunteer coordinator, Julia Martin, and the organization's lead trainer, Rachel Levy, pointed out that Muslims are not the only targets of hateful speech and violence. According to their website, by teaching Bystander Intervention and Organizing 101 classes across the city, the group is able to combat racism as well as Islamophobia while empowering concerned citizens to help out any marginalized person they see being mistreated.

The comprehensive training class I attended was a major eye-opener. When I signed up, I was impressed by how easy it was to schedule and by the fact that it was priced on a donation basis. Upon my arrival, I was struck all the more by the kind and forward-thinking environment created by the teachers. At the start, we were asked our preferred pronouns, and it was made clear that we should not assume anyone else's gender, ethnicity, or level of ability.

The kindness, inclusion, and intelligence of the approach taken by AAANY and The Accompany Project seems to be completely at the forefront of intersectionality and social justice.

In learning how to stand up for myself and others, it was helpful to gain a better understanding of how the intersectionality of class, gender, ethnicity, race, and so on can give way to overlapping forms of disadvantage and discrimination. So too was embracing the idea that the actions we take on behalf of one another, like walking with someone in places that cause them fear, is central to social justice. Such concepts stuck out for me, as did the empowerment that comes from a small shift in vocabulary, from *victim* to *survivor*.

Through the training, I discovered how much power we all have to change situations that might ordinarily make us feel powerless. The class started with exercises that sharpened our ability to read body language, connecting us at the same time to how our own bodies can communicate more confidently and authoritatively—whether we're in fight-or-flight mode or not. We talked openly about all the reasons why we stay bystanders instead of becoming *upstanders* and actually intervene. Fortunately, however, the training went on to give us many tools for doing more than merely standing by.

Prompts for remembering effective intervention options were reviewed as the four *Ds—Direct*, *Delegate*, *Distract*, and *Delay*—along with a discussion of the many ways they can be applied. We were also taught several verbal de-escalation strategies.

Rachel Levy emphasizes that it's advisable to name the "specific behavior that is inappropriate." Rather than sounding oppositional, she adds, it's a good idea to foster a sense of unity by referring to yourself and the perpetrator as "we." Each strategy provides guidance on ways to speak or behave that Rachel says can "safely disrupt a hostile or aggressive situation you may witness and . . . ensure your actions are more helpful than harmful."

The Accompany Project was born from the kindness that I've learned can help defuse—and ultimately overcome—hateful, threatening rhetoric. Knowing others have your back is enough to let you know that, yes, you too can find the courage to be an upstanding citizen on behalf of someone who doesn't feel safe.

Josh's story about bravely standing up for strangers in the face of hate is further proof that we all need to channel kindness and look out for one another. No one should ever be bullied or discriminated against for being who they are. I don't put up with it any time I see it, online or in person—and you shouldn't, either. To take a bystander intervention training in New York, check out The Accompany Project; or to promote inclusiveness and love in your own neighborhood, check out Hate Has No Home Here.

Lady Gaga

JOSH GREENBLATT

As we all spread the word, it's so encouraging to know that the adjustments we learn to make in our own neighborhoods are the kinds of changes in mindset that can shift the entire world.

21

Only with CONSENT

EM HOGGETT

Acquaintance rape was not a term that Californian Jasmin Enriquez had ever heard until one day in a women's studies class at Pennsylvania State University, when a visiting lecturer presented startling statistics about its prevalence. The presenter discussed the fact that 90 percent of rape survivors personally knew their rapist before the assault occurred. Jasmin also learned that because many don't know what to call what's happened to them, acquaintance rape often goes unreported.

Sitting in class that day, a light bulb went off for her. In high school, Jasmin had been forced to have sex with someone she thought loved her. Afterward, she couldn't understand what had happened. She knew that she felt disgusting, that something felt wrong "in her bones," but she didn't know why. She couldn't speak to anyone about it, fearing she would be judged for going against her Catholic values by having sex before marriage—even though the act had been without her consent.

"I never imagined I would be *raped*. I thought that happened to people who were walking down the street, not something that could happen by someone who loved you," she explained.

Attempting to put the trauma behind her, Jasmin eagerly went off to her dream college, where she soon developed a friendship with a young man she trusted—someone whom she believed cared for her. Much to her shock, one night at a fraternity house, for the second time in her life, she was raped—again, an act that she still didn't have the knowledge to name.

Jasmin felt traumatized by both situations but didn't have answers as to how they could have happened, let alone why. Finally, in that moment of realization in her women's studies class, she was able to identify the rapes for what they were. Both times, she had fallen into the 90-percent category of people who experience acquaintance rape.

She knew right away that a broader conversation had to happen and resolved to play an active role in getting more people to talk about sexual assault—starting with her own campus. Though she hadn't intended to start a club, she sort of stumbled onto the idea that a campus group of some sort could better collaborate with the college's student government to get out the word about activities and awareness building. Fittingly, Jasmin named the club Only With Consent and quickly began to mobilize, organizing events around improving communication and educating all students about sexual assault and consent on campus.

After she graduated in 2014, under her guidance, Only With Consent became an official nonprofit with the goal of creating a far-reaching system that educates people on consent, from infancy to adulthood. Jasmin's passion is contagious. She insists,

"I want to teach about consent in schools and reinforce it in the community. I want it to be a conversation. I want people to become passionate about asking their partner for consent."

Her vision includes raising children with an understanding of their own bodily anatomy, teaching them age-appropriate consent language, and encouraging parents to educate their kids about consent. Consent education, she says, ought to continue from birth to college, into the workplace, and beyond.

You are never too young or too old to have safe boundaries.

She emphasizes, "It's a problem most people don't understand or talk about openly. I think it's necessary that everyone get an education about consent, regardless of age, background, anything. The best-case scenario is that we educate every single person about consent."

In all communities, and in most circles, Jasmin has found that the conversations about acquaintance rape and the right to say no are long overdue. The response has been positive. "Most people say they wish they had this message when they were younger."

Currently, Only With Consent—run by Jasmin, together with her husband, Mike—works with universities, teaching workshops, giving presentations, and collaborating on awareness events. They also have footprints in communities concerned about keeping all citizens safe—whether in relationships, in homes, or on the street—and have taken part in major public events like Comic Con and San Diego Pride.

At every step of her journey to prevent and end sexual assault, Jasmin has encountered countless others who, like her, felt something wrong after a sexual experience to which they didn't consent. As a youth reporter working with the Born This Way Foundation, I am no exception. The term *acquaintance rape* was one I'd never heard, either, and when I had an experience similar to Jasmin's, I went for months without knowing what had actually happened to me.

When the opportunity came up to interview Jasmin for a profile in kindness and bravery, I leaped at it. As fellow survivors, both working to spread awareness of sexual assault, we have much in common and know there is more work to do.

Over the phone, Jasmin and I wondered, *How many other people are out there who have been raped and do not even know it?*

We talked about both women and men who feel a sense of self-loathing and confusion over their experience, with no understanding as to why they feel as they do.

We talked about a very public turning point for survivors that occurred at the 2016 Oscars, when Lady Gaga sang "Til It Happens to You"—the song she cowrote with Diane Warren for the 2015 documentary *The Hunting Ground*, which exposes widespread problems of sexual assault on college campuses. As a survivor of sexual abuse herself, Lady Gaga included fifty fellow survivors onstage with her at the Oscars, which went on to bring down the house.

Among those fifty fellow survivors was Jasmin Enriquez. Naturally, I was curious to know how she ended up on that stage for such a pivotal moment. She told me that after being interviewed in *The Hunting Ground*, the community involved in the film stayed in touch, supporting one another and working together to amplify the discussion. "So," she elaborated, "when the Oscars were approaching, the team reached out to us to ask if we wanted to take part."

She was honored and said yes without hesitation.

My questions for Jasmin continued.

CHANNEL KINDNESS: What was the main thing you took from the Oscars?

JASMIN: That there are so many people who have a story. It was one of the first times I felt not alone in what I was going through, in a public space, and I hoped that through that, other people realized that they're not alone and that there's a community out there that supports them, too.

CHANNEL KINDNESS: What other advice would you give survivors who are struggling to cope?

JASMIN: The most helpful thing for me personally is trying to remind myself to have self-compassion along the way.

She added that everyone has their own means of finding methods for self-healing.

For her, cooking is very therapeutic. Hobbies, outlets like exercise, and being in nature, as well as therapy or finding someone with a good ear are all constructive steps to take. She has also found that joining a local group that helps educate others about the issues of sexual abuse can be lifesaving.

CHANNEL KINDNESS: Any advice for survivors who want to heal through some sort of creative outlet or launching their own nonprofit?

JASMIN: Just start with whatever feels right for you. Take it one day at a time. Start where you feel moved, and it'll grow as you express yourself. You might share it with friends or community. Just do what feels right. When I share my story, I feel like I'm connecting to others. I always remind myself that I'm doing Only With Consent to help myself and help others along the way.

CHANNEL KINDNESS: Do you suggest that survivors speak out about their experience as a way of healing?

JASMIN: Do whatever feels right for you. Some people can't speak out for different reasons. Most important, I want them to know they're not alone and it's not their fault. I wouldn't say there's a right or wrong way to go about it. . . . We are in a community together, and we all want to see each other be okay and succeed.

To anyone who has experienced sexual assault, **you are brave**. Getting through every day can sometimes be difficult, and that in itself is an **act of bravery**.

We ended the interview by talking about how Jasmin relates to bravery and kindness. She wanted very much to send the message "to anyone who has experienced sexual assault, *you are brave*. Getting through every day can sometimes be difficult, and that in itself is an act of bravery." As for kindness, Jasmin followed up by saying, "If you have experienced sexual assault, be kind to yourself, know it wasn't your fault. I didn't treat myself well for a long time—it took me a long time to take care of my body and understand I deserve to be healthy and deserve love; I deserve things I had convinced myself I didn't."

Jasmin's journey as the head of a nonprofit may have come about by accident, as she says. However, it seems she was truly meant to do this work, to remind each of us that knowledge is power and that consent is ours and ours alone to give.

Em, thank you for shedding light on this important and not often enough discussed topic. I want to underscore what you said—**you are never too young or too old to have safe boundaries**. According to Rape, Abuse & Incest National Network (RAINN), approximately 11.2% of all undergraduate and graduate students experience rape or sexual assault through physical force, violence, or incapacitation. I am heartbroken that Jasmin had to endure this trauma but grateful to her for starting Only with Consent to work toward ensuring that it doesn't happen to another person. Thank you for including *The Hunting Ground* in your story; I was very proud of the brave women who shared their stories in that film. To learn more about the roles we can all play in stopping sexual assault, you can visit RAINN.

Lady Gaga

22

A WAKE-UP CALL TO ACTION

BROOKE A. GOLDMAN

4:30 A.M.

My sister, Ava, and I woke with hearts racing and the promise of observing a new, untouched world. This was the morning of our long-awaited departure, and we felt the urgency of a mission we had been planning for two years.

Ava and I were about to become the first teens on record to fly from New York to Newtok, a remote Alaskan village caught in the grips of the direct results of climate change. Many people, even in Alaska's main cities, remain unaware of Newtok's struggle with relocation. Because it is remote and poorly publicized, the opportunity to travel there is rare.

How did this day come about? How did Ava, age seventeen, and I, age fifteen, decide to make this journey? What were we intent on learning from this visit and sharing with others? Where did our interest in the village of Newtok begin?

Interestingly enough, our connection to all inhabitants of Alaska's coastal villages dates back to a time in childhood when we received the gift of a cookbook, of all things, from our great-aunt. It was called *The Shishmaref Day School Class of 1973 Eskimo Cookbook*, a flimsy thin paperback of rumpled pages that changed my life.

Shishmaref today, about 370 miles north of Newtok, is a poster child for climate-forced relocation. A village built on ice that is now vanishing, it will rapidly be uninhabitable. But when we were little girls, to us, it was an unspoiled spot on the map that offered food items like "Eskimo Ice Cream" and had other preparations of meals totally unlike those we were raised with.

"Skin the seal, boil the blubber . . . " we read, our eyes wide with wonder. Adding salt was about as flavorful as any of it got.

The recipes, vastly different from our own, left in our imaginations an indelible mark of curiosity and excitement that made us eager to follow stories of the real-life characters living in a world away from us. We felt as if we got to know the people personally. The expressions of pride and love they had for their land tugged at our hearts, drawing us closer to the villagers, connecting us so much that they didn't seem so distant.

Later, when we first heard of the Shishmaref relocation plight, we asked ourselves how families within the same country we inhabit could face problems so different from anything we had to confront. We had to do something. We had to help tell their story, and not just what was happening to the people of Shishmaref but also to the many other villagers up and down Alaska's coasts who are now facing the harshest of realities.

So, for those two years before our planned expedition, we spent our time doing extensive research, and that was how we came across the looming crisis for the people of Newtok. Surrounding the village on three of its sides is the Ninglick River. For years the river has eaten away at the land, sweeping it away forever with the tide, which empties into the Bering Sea. As temperatures rapidly increase, the permafrost underneath Newtok has continued to thaw. This has resulted in the erosion of approximately one hundred feet of land every year, pushing the water's edge ever closer to villagers.

From Romy Cadiente, Newtok's village relocation coordinator, we learned that cemeteries, schools, and houses will be swept away in only a few years. Other villages also struggling with the rising threat of relocation have turned to seawalls to add time to their race against nature. However, Newtok is too fragile and low-lying for the seawalls to hold.

This is not a question of *if* but rather of *when*. And when the land is overtaken by water, everyone's lives will be in danger. Relocation to a new village is actually the only choice Newtok has.

Even before we arrived in Alaska, the pending trauma of Newtok's relocation led me to realize that the villagers are being forced to become refugees—not of war but of climate change.

The more we learned, the more Ava and I felt a bond with Newtok that motivated us to do something bold and attention-getting, if only to raise awareness of the crisis. How many even know that whole villages are being forced to move due to weather-induced changes? It's a clear warning of what's to come in our collective future—a perilous fate if we don't start to become better prepared.

The way I see it, society has to work its way back to start erasing the damage we created in order to move forward. And the first step in accomplishing that is to become educated. To that end, Ava and I decided to chronicle the story of our trip to Newtok in a documentary.

The moment when our plane touched down in Anchorage, Alaska, Ava and I exchanged looks of nervous anticipation. We were about to meet many of the people we'd come to know only through emails and phone calls. We wasted little time in moving forward with a series of interviews. It didn't take long to find out that all we had studied from afar was very real.

"The heat and rising sea levels have been making my salmon take different routes," one local told us. "Me and my buddy . . . now we need to travel far from home to go to different streams. The gas money for the travel . . . you know, it all counts."

The seriousness of climate change was definitely on the radar of the Alaskan youth we met. "I thought about not having kids because I don't want them to grow up in a world where it's so uncertain because of climate change," said Alex Jorgensen, Arctic Youth Ambassador.

The thought occurred to me—it is this uncertainty in weather that frightens so many, understandably so, and what drives my initiative. If we know that weather uncertainty is uncontrollable, let's focus our energy on something we can control. Our preparedness.

From Anchorage, we flew to Bethel, and from there, we chartered a small nine-seater propeller plane to Newtok—where the most welcoming faces greeted my sister and me along with our team. They were visibly excited by our presence and by the fact that somehow two teens from Manhattan cared deeply about the ancestral land their Yupik culture was built upon.

ATVs (all-terrain vehicles) picked us up from the airstrip. We drove on uneven planks of wood that acted as narrow roads atop the pervasive mud, just wide enough for the ATVs to traverse. As we drove, everyone waved to us. The air was clear and we were able to observe that the nearby water's edge was being held back by only a limp wall of eroded land.

Romy let us film a presentation he gave about the ominous erosion of the Alaskan coastline. Pointing to visuals on the screen, he said, "It may look like a map to you, but that flooding is right outside this door right here."

Even though relocation is the only option for Newtok, the largest logistical problem is that the price tag for the villagers to move all at once to their new village of Mertarvik is far too steep. A report by the US Army Corps of Engineers concluded that it would cost upward of $80 million or more. Nine miles away, Mertarvik sits atop a dark volcanic rock on Nelson Island. During the winter months, getting there will take approximately thirty minutes by snowmobile, and, of course, the trek involves crossing the Ninglick River.

Fortunately, because it was summer when we visited, Ava and I were able to travel the nine miles by boat. We witnessed construction crews working on the first phase of infrastructure—running water, a sewer system, and six new homes. Working against the clock, a big push for construction has to happen in summer, as the colder months bring brutal storms and water levels that rapidly rise.

All of this has spelled enormous trouble for the residents of Newtok, but they're not alone in their worry. Nor is the crisis confined to Alaska. According to reports by the US Geological Survey (USGS), Louisiana is losing its coastline at the rate of one football field every one hundred minutes. Not only that, but NPR reports that more than half of the state's population lives on the coast. States like Massachusetts, California, Texas, and Florida, as well as many countries outside of the US, are struggling with the same issues. Nonprofit organization Climate Central projected that the greatest sea level increase will occur on the shores of New York City. Significant storm surges, such as 2012's Hurricane Sandy, will become more frequent and more impactful.

We tend to assume that whatever happens weather-wise in a location as far away as the Arctic could never directly impact our weather. Not so. In fact, in early 2014, frigid air from the Arctic traveled to the Northern Hemisphere, causing extreme weather in multiple places, creating fifty daily record low temperatures on January 6 alone. Today, the Arctic continues to warm two times faster than the global average. What this is doing to the rest of the planet must not only be recognized but action must be taken. It's a fact that climate-induced relocation is the extreme result of the weather shifts occurring around the world.

The documentary that Ava and I set out to make, *CLIMIGRATION: Our Generation's Battle*, is helping others learn about the issue and how it impacts communities across the globe. Because we were raised to care about the fate of those different from us—through an obscure cookbook given to us as children, no less—this for us is a labor of love. The message of our mission to Newtok is clear, but equally important is our emphasis on how we all have to get involved, however we can.

Thank you for sharing this beautiful part of the world with us, Brooke, and for all that you and your sister, Ava, are doing to help it thrive for future generations. Your enthusiasm and passion to protect the environment remind us that being kind includes being kind to the planet. I hope this story inspires us all to go green—recycle, plant a tree, green your commute, or reduce your carbon footprint. To watch Brooke's documentary and support her climigration project, check out her nonprofit, Climigrate; and for more information about protecting and conserving the environment, visit Greenpeace or 350.org.

Lady Gaga

It is my generation that most needs to see what's happening in Alaska as a wake-up call for action. We need to be informed about extreme weather preparedness and not wait for another crisis to occur for it to become yet another cry for help.

My sister and I feel so passionate about stimulating change to create a safer world for our generation that, in addition to our documentary, we created climigrate.org—a nonprofit that seeks to educate at-risk populations on *climigration* (the forced migration of a population due to climate change).

One of our most important goals now is to raise money for the people of Newtok so they can move safely to Mertarvik. Once they were a tiny village that resembled another spot on the Alaska coast, known to us only for its seal-flavored Eskimo Ice Cream and other local delicacies. But now, as part of our human family, they are in desperate need of relocation funding, and we can't turn away without doing all that we can to help.

By taking action, we are putting kindness to work, proving that age is no barrier to action nor an excuse for inaction when it comes to caring for all who live on this earth, the only home we have.

23

INTERNATIONAL *Day* OF SELF~LOVE

SANAH JIVANI

I would like to tell you that the toughest day of my life began the morning I woke up to find all my hair on my pillow. But that was not really the toughest day of my life.

It was definitely soul-crushing, though—a sight I'll never forget. The mere thought of getting out of bed overwhelmed me. Even more terrifying was the idea of looking at myself in the mirror. When I finally did muster the strength to face the mirror, I could barely stand, let alone breathe. Fear and self-hatred immediately filled my being.

Will I ever be able to truly love myself again?

It was a long time before I could answer that, but I was soon diagnosed with alopecia universalis, an autoimmune condition that causes complete hair loss. My immediate reaction was to rush out and purchase a wig to hide the condition. The last thing I wanted was for anyone to see what I saw in the mirror that morning.

When I walked into school for the first time after my diagnosis, it seemed rumors instantly began to spread about why I was wearing a wig. The bullying was endless, cruel and, well, original. From gum in my wig to a note in my locker with the words *50 Ways to Go Kill Yourself*, I was heartbroken in every way. Some kids even created an online page to make fun of me, posting status updates with still more guesses as to why I was wearing a wig.

More and more days stood in as candidates for Worst Day Ever until one particular afternoon, by chance, I noticed something that made my bleak day slightly better. All this time, people had been saying mean things to me, but the things I said to myself were ten times worse. Every day I would come home, look in the mirror, and add to the bullying that was already going on.

Was self-bullying a real thing? Apparently for me, it was. In that moment of realization,

I knew the first step in getting past my insecurity was learning to be kinder to myself. For starters, I consciously looked for ways to practice self-love and self-care. The investment *in myself, by myself* slowly but surely paid off. Once I learned to love and stand up for myself, the bullying really died down. My worth had nothing to do with what hair was on my head, and in a way, the fact that I had lived through such a hard passage and was dealing with the reality of my diagnosis made me feel bravely beautiful for who I am as a strong person. With that understanding, finally, I could feel at peace with myself, and it was a joy I had never before experienced.

Then, another powerful realization struck me: I wanted to share this joy with others. Though I wasn't sure how, I had a quirky idea that was hard to shake. What if, I wondered, there was a day where people could truly appreciate themselves? What if there was a day when we did not have to feel tied down by insecurities? What if there was a day that had nothing to do with other people validating us but everything to do with our own self-validation?

With those thoughts, I developed the framework for the International Day of Self-Love—a day that lets us feel free to be ourselves. I decided to designate the celebration to be held on February 13, the day before Valentine's Day; after all, it's important to love and appreciate *you* before investing in others.

Since developing the concept in 2011, this day has spread to more than a hundred schools in twenty-eight countries, reaching more than fifty thousand students. Schools that participate in the International Day of Self-Love receive free curriculum materials to help with building the skills of loving oneself. Often for the first time, students are taught the important practices of self-love and self-care.

In 2018, a school in Bloomington, Illinois, decided to dress in "YOU-niforms"—plain white shirts on which students wrote an insecurity. Throughout the day, their peers wrote kind comments on their shirts to help them accept and embrace the quality they feel most insecure about. How amazing and inspiring. A school in Westerville, Ohio, decided that their theme one year was "Grow in Confidence." They crafted a large tree in the cafeteria, where each leaf symbolized a strength of a student.

A school in New York City decided to put an encouraging sticky note on each door, locker, window, and wall. They wanted to make sure students felt encouraged and inspired in every way.

How can I begin to decide what has been the best day of my life so far? The contest will be between last year's International Day of Self-Love and next year's. I only hope it continues to grow every year, ultimately becoming a holiday that will someday be printed on every calendar around the globe.

Why not?

Never second-guess the power of an idea that channels kindness.

♥

When we talk about kindness, we often forget to talk about kindness to ourselves. For me, being kind to myself includes cooking, meditating, playing with my dogs, and being surrounded by friends and family. It's not easy to learn how to be kind to yourself and to find a habit of self-love, and I applaud Sanah for learning to love herself. You are worthy of love, Sanah. We all are. We are all beautiful inside and out, and I encourage you to take a moment to write three things you love about yourself in the space below, and if you'd like to support Sanah in her mission to spread self-love, visit International Natural Day.

Lady Gaga

24

LEARNING TO LIVE LIFE AS IS

PERRI EASLEY

The most anxious time of my life crashed around me in the middle of the eleventh grade. Even though I'd been warned that junior year is the year that counts, I didn't know how bad the pressure could be until it happened.

Part of it is external. Students are constantly reminded that eleventh grade is one of the last times colleges and universities can see academic excellence. We hear how imperative it is to take a rigorous course load and also achieve high grades. On top of that, we have extracurriculars and other commitments vying for our time.

The other part is internal—at least, it is for many of us who place high demands on ourselves. That's who I had always been. People usually saw me as an accomplished go-getter and a bubbly, energetic girl, never seen without a smile on her face, someone who was always confident and upbeat. Deep down, I knew that wasn't the full story, but my ultra-happy, super-confident image was something I never tried to change.

The pressure from outside and from within drained me—to the point where I no longer felt like myself at all. Even as I sank into what was soon unmistakably depression, I continued to hide behind my usual façade of happiness. The mask felt safer, offering some security despite being detrimental to my true well-being. So I played that part well, and I continued to suppress my true feelings and my worry that deep down I was becoming an unhappy, stressed-out girl who always wanted more and who could never simply live her life *as is*.

Growing up, the truth is that I'd never been able to accept myself *as is*. Instead I had to be smarter, prettier, more personable, better. This drive to achieve may have motivated me to strive for excellence, but by junior year it had taken a tremendous toll on my disposition and overall well-being.

Everyone noticed changes in me—my teachers, my family members, and my circle of friends and supporters. Even I saw a change in myself. Before long, I had to admit that it was time to seek some assistance.

Two months before the end of the school year, I was officially diagnosed with depression. It did not come as a surprise, though. Something was wrong because I had lost touch with who I was, so if I was depressed, I had to hope that knowing there was a name for it would help me get to solid ground again. Or that's what I tried to tell myself as I struggled to come to grips with my depression.

The more I focused on what was wrong with me, the harder it became to find anything that was right with me. As noted by the National Alliance on Mental Illness, some of the most common signs of depression are trouble sleeping, moody behavior, and abnormal eating patterns. These symptoms, however, are often attributed to the typical stressed-out, overworked teenager. No one seemed to know or be able to tell me if this was just part of my presumed "teenage angst" or if it represented something larger. Answers were not fast in coming.

Complicating matters was the fact that in my community, depression and other mental illnesses were not widely accepted topics of conversation. Not only that, but it's my sense that mental health services are not properly illuminated in minority communities, and especially not in communities of color. As an African American girl, I'd been raised to think that having depression simply wasn't an option—at least, it was never brought up or mentioned as a possibility.

An ongoing inner dialogue didn't help:

What's wrong with me? Am I just weak or too emotionally incapable of dealing with stressful situations?

Depression, I discovered over time, can be eased by learning new coping mechanisms—say, meditation and yoga. Awareness of the issues and triggers can be helpful. I've had to embrace the truth that I'm on a journey toward accepting myself without having to prove to others that I'm always—and only—a happy, bubbly go-getter.

Things have gotten better. While my situation is still not ideal, I've learned to accept that I am not perfect but *I am good enough*. I learned that year—which I did survive—to accept that I was a seventeen-year-old African American girl living with depression. And going forward, I can continue to learn to live my life simply *as is*.

The most liberating lesson happened in a moment when it dawned on me that I wasn't alone in this quest. That awareness, combined with my growing self-acceptance, inspired me to create a social movement with a mental wellness component. The social movement is simply called As Is.

As Is wants to see mental health at the forefront of societal issues. In recent years, there has been a record-breaking increase of mental illnesses in young people, which includes depression, eating disorders, and anxiety, among other illnesses. While it is evident that mental health is a pressing issue in today's world, its stigma slows down widespread reform. Therefore, As Is works to expand access to mental health services for the average American, to recognize and address the intersectionality of mental illnesses. What that means, for example, is understanding how factors such as race and gender bias, or other forms of exclusion, impact minority communities when it comes to getting help. The goal is to provide appropriate accommodations for mental health patients in a professional and/or academic setting and, ultimately, eliminate the stigma of mental health issues.

In this piece, Perri writes about how empowering it can be to share your mental health story, and I want to celebrate her bravery for doing so. I have found so much healing and community when I share my own journey. Please remember that there is no shame in saying you're struggling; as I've said many times, it's okay to not be okay. If you're still surrounded by mental health stigma (as far too many of us are), check out the Seize the Awkward campaign to get the conversation started, and for more information as to how to learn to talk openly and honestly about your mental health with your friends and family, visit The Jed Foundation.

Lady Gaga

The beauty of a social movement is that it grows from the roots up, through word of mouth. Soon after I began to articulate my vision—in person and online—I heard from dozens of people in my community who wanted to be part of an As Is movement. We have been growing organically ever since. Our vision is based on the notion that with greater and necessary attention toward mental health, we will see a fairer and healthier country.

Our movement is open to all, and I encourage you to join the crusade to make mental health conversations more prevalent in society. Don't shy away from discussing mental health–related topics at the dinner table. Educate yourself on different mental illnesses. Take a mental health "first aid" course. Use your networks and social media contacts to spread the word, adding a hashtag for #AsIs. Do as much as you can to try to normalize the prevalence of mental health challenges. This will only make the mission of As Is more achievable.

Together, we can illuminate the issues of mental health for a better, more accepting, kinder world. Mental health awareness is always "in."

If I've learned anything, it's the wisdom that accepting ourselves for who we are, as we are, takes bravery and even some risk. We don't have to focus on what's wrong with us when we can choose to embrace what's right with us.

*And guess what? Not everyone has to think you're awesome **as is**. Only you do.*

25
THE HELPING
HANDS OF YOGA

━ JESSICA ZHANG ━

Why didn't I see the signs? What could I have done to help? How could this happen? Why didn't anyone reach out before it was too late?

Those are only a few of the heart-wrenching questions asked by the friends and loved ones of a person, especially one so very young, who has chosen to end their life. For those of us in our teen years, the news that one of our own has died by suicide is devastating and confusing.

When a childhood friend of mine died by suicide in our high school years, I fell into despair, asking myself all those questions and more. Of course, I tried to avoid blaming myself, but I couldn't shake the thoughts of what she must have been thinking and feeling in her last desperate minutes.

From what I understood, my friend had been suffering from severe stress and depression, although most people didn't know it. Mental health issues aren't commonly discussed in my community. Besides, in this competitive culture, it's been ingrained in us to disregard people who casually talk about self-harm and depression. The demand to excel in not only academics but also extracurriculars is extreme—from societal, romantic, and familial pressures and, obviously, from peer pressure.

When I talked with other friends, I was reminded that many of the typical symptoms exhibited by someone who is suicidal also occur with what many people see as just being stressed. Still, that didn't keep me from thinking, *If only I'd supported her more, if only I'd let her know that I cared for her, she wouldn't have had to resort to such extreme ends.*

A feeling of hopelessness and dejection settled over me as the weeks went on. The reality is that mental health crises ending in suicide happen in schools all over my district and in other cities near Silicon Valley, where I'm from. The fact that her death wasn't an isolated tragedy continued to trouble me. Worse was the fact that the pattern kept repeating itself. During my sister's junior year of high school, a student she knew died by suicide by jumping off the Golden Gate Bridge in San Francisco.

The same questions had been asked: Why didn't anyone see the signs? We heard that, in her case, not unlike many others, my sister's friend had become too burdened by doing well in school and in outside academic competitions.

After my friend died by suicide, I looked for a way to process my feelings and release the negative energies that seemed to grip my body and my being. The practices of yoga and mindfulness gave me a much-needed outlet, allowing me to suddenly feel more clear-headed—with a new desire to make a change. Every day at home, I began to practice at 6:00 a.m., before getting ready for school; every night, I meditated before I went to sleep. Whenever a problem or obstacle came my way, instead of holding in my emotions or reacting to stress, I developed a routine that let me breathe the concerns out and imagine them gently floating away.

In all candor, I had once seen yoga as a relaxing sport, more or less. After settling into a routine with my practice, I realized the true reason others seek out the ancient practice of yoga—for solace, healing, and renewal. As I grew stronger and more knowledgeable about different forms of yoga, I couldn't help wondering whether I might be able to share the benefits with others in my community.

In particular, I had to believe there was a way to disrupt the continual cycle of kids thinking it's okay—because they assume it's the norm—to constantly be stressed. Experts tell us that the level of pressure young people are combatting is not normal at all and that there is an urgent need to end the vicious cycle of suicide among teens and young adults.

Instead of waiting for the next tragedy and wondering what we could have done to prevent it, I founded a traveling yoga studio with my sister, a certified RYT 200 yoga instructor (as well as a teacher at Yoga Alliance). We were similarly motivated, having both lost friends to suicide, having both seen and experienced firsthand how it feels to be a student in a high-pressure community, and having both observed how the community seemed, to us, somewhat indifferent just weeks after the incidents.

Knowing we wanted to expose children and teens to the practice of yoga by volunteering in schools and communities in and around Silicon Valley, I started the effort by teaching elementary school students basic yoga poses and breathing techniques. My sister and I tried our best to turn the rowdy, mischievous kids whose energy was positively infectious into quiet, calm individuals—not always successfully, especially when they were in the final resting pose of Savasana. Then we brought the free yoga classes to our local library, where people of all ages in the community could participate in yoga and mindfulness trainings.

Our nonprofit, Yoga4youths, has opened so many opportunities for us to create lasting collaborations with different schools and community hubs in our area. As we tackle a range of problems that plague our community (not only mental health issues), we have redefined "youth" by inviting people of all ages, races, socioeconomic backgrounds, religions, genders, sexual orientations, and beliefs to our free classes.

As soon as they walk through the door, they're given a safe haven where love and unity give them permission to leave their emotional baggage—and their shoes—outside the studio. We cultivate an atmosphere that is personal and welcoming for all levels of yogis but especially for beginners who have never tried yoga or mindfulness before.

Our mission, as Yoga4youths grows, is to remain a student-run nonprofit that teaches free yoga lessons to economically disadvantaged elementary, middle, and high school students, with the ultimate goal of operating across the nation. In addition to using yoga as a tool to address the mental well-being of young elementary students ages five to eleven by teaching them yoga, another priority is to mobilize teenagers to exercise more and gain the leadership skills of teaching younger kids.

My sincere hope is to never again have members of my community or others bury a young person who took their own life and ask, *Why didn't we do more?* By teaching yoga to young people, I believe we are giving them the tools to combat stress—arming their young minds to step onto the mat and learn how to be strong, both mentally and physically.

Our motto, "Minds Over Mats," can influence the next generation to be mindful and more clear-headed in their decision-making, from monumental, life-altering opportunities to the everyday choices.

On our mats, **we can** educate one another on the very fundamental need of the human experience: love, which is the opposite of hate, stress, anxiety, loss, depression, insecurity, and fear. We can let go of demands on ourselves to be perfect at everything and **simply aspire to be good, kind, and brave**.

In whatever way possible, I'll continue to use my role as a teacher to share the message that every life is precious and everyone is worth fighting for. No matter what difficulties and obstacles you may face, whether they're predetermined or born out of your environment, they can be remedied through less drastic or permanent measures than suicide. And although it may not seem like it, you never have to go through difficult times alone, because there are always people who want to be there for you, talk to you, and support you.

If you do spot problematic signs from a stressed-out friend or someone feeling overwhelmed, you might encourage that person to join you on the mat. I know yoga is not the cure-all for suicidal thoughts or depression, but it can be a good start in helping us all become more aware of these thoughts and feelings both in ourselves and in others. You will be amazed at the different kinds of people you'll meet right next to you, doing the Downward Dog pose or the Warrior Stance or just smiling with tears of release and relief falling from their eyes.

JESSICA ZHANG

♥

Our mental health is just as important as our physical health, and they go hand in hand—we cannot have one without the other. I am so proud that Jessica is helping others remember that message through yoga and meditation; two practices that I have found very useful in my own life. If you're in the Silicon Valley area and want to learn more about Jessica's organization, visit Yoga4Youths, and for resources on how to be kind to your mind, check out Mindful. And if you or someone you know is struggling with suicidal ideation, please reach out to the National Suicide Prevention Lifeline to connect with a trained crisis counselor.

Lady Gaga

26

CANINES
FOR
COMMUNITY

JESSICA MORALES

As a native of Coral Springs and Parkland in Florida, I know every member of my community was forever altered by the February 14 school shooting that took seventeen lives, turning a sunny Valentine's Day morning at Marjory Stoneman Douglas High School (MSD) into the deadliest high school shooting in United States' history. Though time has moved on, grief remains. Yet, through the tragedy, we as a community came together in powerful, unforgettable ways to help one another with the healing process.

The day that students, teachers, and staff returned to school, two weeks after the shooting, first responders and many from the community were present to offer support. Also out in numbers was a special brigade from the Humane Society of Broward County (HSBC). The HSBC's Canines for Community Resilience Program in Fort Lauderdale seeks to provide joy, healing, and love by bringing therapy animals to those in need. Partnered with almost every organization in Broward County, the Canines for Community Resilience Program works directly with the school board, hospitals, rehab facilities, nursing homes, and libraries and offers specialized volunteer and dog team programs for new potential therapy animals.

As a youth reporter for Channel Kindness, I had the honor of interviewing the canine program's manager, Marni Bellavia, an avid animal lover whose sidekick in life is Karma, her miniature Australian shepherd. When I sat down to interview Marni—with Karma sitting patiently at her side—I asked how the dogs had become so closely connected to MSD. Marni explained that when experts began to organize a safe return for those who would be coming back (not everyone chose to return), she was immediately moved to get the Canines for Community Resilience dogs involved in welcoming the students back to campus and helping to heal a shaken community.

"Within just a few blocks of MSD, there are several elementary and middle schools," she reminded me. "Because they didn't catch the shooter right away, students as young as five and six years old had to evacuate the same way—with their hands in the air, on shoulders—and had to hide underneath desks. It's a very traumatic situation for the teenagers, let alone for the young elementary school students."

The dogs seemed to understand the gravity of the moment as they waited together to be among the first new faces students encountered while returning to MSD and the surrounding schools. The dogs were taken as well to help heal the first responders, the 911 dispatchers, and those injured at hospitals, and they also provided comfort to grieving families at funerals and vigils for the seventeen lives lost. Some MSD students who were at first too traumatized to talk about the incident gravitated toward the dogs and found themselves talking to the dogs about their experience. Others, who couldn't open up, silently grieved, with the therapy dogs comforting them at their sides or sitting in their laps. Some of the human guardians of the dogs remarked that sitting in laps wasn't something they normally liked to do.

Animals, understood to have heightened powers of emotional intelligence and empathy that we have yet to fully measure, play a key role in healing for trauma survivors attempting to move forward. Without words, they provide unconditional love and devotion. They make it okay to grieve, to be quiet and still.

HSBC's Animal Assisted Therapy Program is not only limited to providing therapy dogs. Cats, birds, ferrets, guinea pigs, rabbits, horses, donkeys, and pot-bellied pigs are also part of the program. The HSBC proudly sent an emergency response team of twenty Canines for Community Resilience dogs, free of charge, to every school, organization, or group that was in need after the MSD tragedy.

"You feel really good about having somebody say, 'Thank you for bringing your dog. Thank you for letting that dog provide comfort for us in a time where the thought of healing is so far away that you can't imagine ever being okay again.' To be able to bring in the dogs and interact with the grieving community made me feel like I was part of healing the community, even if it was momentarily," Marni explained.

A year and a half later, fourteen dogs had become a regular part of the MSD campus life—even earning a page in the yearbook the following year. Some were dressed up in doggie bow ties, all fluffed up from the groomers, while some just came as their own shaggy selves to sit for the yearbook photo shoot. Looking into the camera, they almost seemed to grasp their special place in the school's history.

You never think a tragedy like this can happen in your community—until it does. It's unexpected, it shakes you to your core, and for the students and their families, healing can sometimes seem impossible. However, Marni and the Canines for Community Resilience are helping them heal.

We will rise above, but we will never forget.

Together, we are MSD strong.

I will never forget that day either, or the youth-led movement that arose from such tragedy. Thank you, Jessica, for sharing your story. Jessica and her story represent the resilience of the generation that drives the Channel Kindness movement and our work at Born This Way Foundation. We know that in the aftermath of tragedy, there is power in community building. If you or someone you know is struggling with post-traumatic stress, please call the Disaster Distress Helpline for 24-7 assistance, and for more resources as to how to help those impacted by gun violence, visit Brady: United Against Gun Violence or Everytown for Gun Safety.

Lady Gaga

27

CHANGING

THE GAME ON

BULLYING

ABBEY PERL

At first, when I became a gamer, I wasn't so different from a lot of the other kids who are drawn to online gaming. A lot of us know what it feels like to be bullied, picked on, teased, or even harassed. Bullies are pretty predictable with the things they target about you—including whatever your perceived weakness or strength might be, how you look, talk, or walk, where you live, how much money your family has, or who your friends are or aren't.

Bullying has been a part of my life ever since I can remember. No matter where I went, it seemed like I never had a safe space to go. The only place where I could feel comfortable—and relieved—was in the world of online gaming. Whenever I played online video games, I felt at ease, knowing my fellow gamers and I had a lot in common. They were my friends who cared for me and loved playing as much as I did. But the more I played, the more I began to detect the online version of bullying.

How did that work? Well, most of the video games I play have chat options—either voice chat or text chat. This helps smoothly coordinate team-oriented games. Unfortunately, it's this part of gaming culture that gives rise to the same kind of bullying that can happen on the playground, in the halls of school, or on the street. If you're good at the game or you're different from other players—watch out. Comments, digs, and questions can become unavoidable if for some reason you find yourself the center of attention.

How old are you? Where do you live? What do your parents do?

As anonymous or low-profile as I try to be, eventually I'm thrust into the spotlight—not because I want to be there but because my fellow gamers realize that, yeah, I'm different from them.

Oh. Yeah. Got it . . .

Are you a girl?!

It is a little rare to find a girl playing video games, especially the few of us who have the courage to be proud of who we are. In the world of online gaming, though, that immediately changes how you are treated. Once my gender was exposed, the next thing I knew, even more inappropriate questions started to come up—including questions about my relationship status. You would think it would have stopped there, but nope. Once it was out there, I was treated differently all because of my gender.

You'd think that this wouldn't happen with gamers, a lot of whom were bullied themselves, but in a world that's unsupervised, where there are no rules and where it's easy to do and say things without being identified, it happens often that former victims of bullying turn into bullies.

Finally, I came to a crossroad after a very scary incident, when someone tracked down my home address along with the names of my parents, and posted the info online for everyone to see. It made me feel uncomfortable and unsafe.

This was a breaking point for me. After dragging myself through pain and suffering, I decided to make a change. Not just for me, but for all the gamers out there who were being made to feel unsafe while doing something they otherwise loved.

In a reality check moment, I thought long and hard and realized, I had a choice: *Leave the game, or change the game.*

My answer was easy. No way was I going to be pushed into leaving. So my next question was to figure out what I could do to promote change in my online and offline communities.

Hmm. That's when it hit me:

Why not start a movement?

As simple as it sounds, I wanted to be different from other movements and organizations. I wanted to connect and relate to my peers in a way that would attract them to want to do more. After months of hard work and planning, my organization emerged to pave the way for kindness and compassion among all.

Kind Mind Collective—originally Diverse Gaming Coalition—provides kindness curriculum to students and adults across the country. As an organization, we do it this way to get people involved in the movement, without preaching or lecturing but still getting them to think about the values and codes of behavior they might not have considered before. In a space where we all have so much content and so many voices grabbing for attention, it's important to find a way to give people reasons to relate and want to be a part of what you're doing. And we are always coming up with new and exciting ways to do that.

You know I love video games, right, Abbey? I love your story. I love how you took your own pain and experiences and channeled them into creating a world in which you—and so many others—could feel safe. I've also been confronted with the question of leaving the game or changing the game, and I'm grateful you and I both chose to change it. For more resources on how to combat online harassment, check out HeartMob or Kind Mind Collective.

Lady Gaga

Our recent project involves an antibullying comic book that follows Asher, the main character, whose gender is deliberately nonbinary and who is a person of color—two aspects of identity increasingly subjected to bullying these days. With this comic, we hope to tackle such issues that need more attention while promoting mental health, self-care and, most important, kindness.

Overall, I am proud of where I have come since I was a victim of bullying. Unfortunately, bullying does affect people every day. The nonprofit StopBullying.gov asserts that kids who are bullied can feel like they are different, powerless, unpopular, and alone. My feeling is that we need to come together and be stronger than the bullies. Never let a bully drag you down from what you love doing most, because that means the bad guys win. Don't let them stop you from pushing yourself to do what can fundamentally change the game—and the world.

28

THE GOLDEN RULE

PEIGHTON McROBIE

"Kelly Brush . . . !"

During commencement exercises for Middlebury College's class of 2008, the announcement of Kelly Brush's name was received with an instantaneous standing ovation and such thunderous applause that the ceremony had to be paused at length. It was a moment that few present would ever forget—especially Kelly, her family, friends, coaches, and her fellow members of Middlebury's ski team.

Just over two years earlier, on February 18, 2006, during Kelly's sophomore year, a very different kind of moment took place that she would also never forget. As a fierce competitor and an elite athlete in the speed events of alpine ski racing, Kelly had always excelled in a number of sports—gymnastics, soccer, lacrosse, basketball, softball, ice skating, swimming, waterskiing, and, even surfing.

Athletic activity, said Kelly, "was something I loved to do . . . It was a huge part of my life." Competitive skiing was also in her blood, a sport in which her parents and her sister had made names for themselves, too.

As a little girl of seven, Kelly had been termed a "tiger"—so called because of her confidence and hard-charging style on the ski slopes. It was that same grit that distinguished her from the moment she arrived at Middlebury; she was a key contributor her freshman year and already a standout early into her sophomore season. At the Dartmouth Winter Carnival (college ski meets are called "carnivals"), Kelly earned the National

Collegiate Athletic Association (NCAA) career-best eighth place ranking in giant slalom. She went into the Williams Winter Carnival with even higher expectations.

After an impressive finish to her first day, all proceeded promisingly on the second day's race. That is, until the critical moment when she sped over a knoll before catching one ski's edge on a patch of ice. This precipitated a nightmare scenario in which she was catapulted off the course, striking one of the stanchions for a ski lift tower. The accident left her with a collapsed lung, four fractured ribs, and a fractured vertebra in her neck. She was paralyzed from the waist down.

Her lowest point, she recalls, was when news came that she would use a wheelchair for the rest of her life. Kelly immediately thought she would never be able to ski again, which she says "was sort of terrifying for me, when I felt like that was the case."

When Kelly's name was announced at graduation, the uproar and standing O was not one of pity but rather of admiration and inspiration. Somehow, in the midst of her fear, at her lowest point, **she summoned the tiger within herself to make it through the horribly painful process** of recovering from hours and hours of surgery, months of physical therapy, countless hospital visits, and having to miss an entire semester of school. Her grit was fueled by the love, kindness, and support of family, friends, and her college community.

Kelly applied the same discipline she'd used in training for sports to her rehabilitation process. "I wasn't really discouraged," she explains. Her focus was always on what was the next thing. As in: "What do I have to do next?"

While Kelly was in rehab, she was introduced to adaptive sports—competitive sports for persons with disabilities that have modified rules and equipment to meet the needs of participants. She remembers, "I was able to get my hands on a hand cycle for the first time when I was in rehab. And it was amazing, I felt so great . . ." Her eyes were opened to the reality that her life wasn't over and her dreams, while maybe in need of some adapting, were still attainable.

There was a problem, however, that she was frustrated to discover: Adaptive sports equipment is extremely expensive. "After you have an injury like this, you already have a higher cost of living, and then the idea of having to spend a couple thousand dollars to get a piece of equipment you really need is so hard for so many people."

Knowing how important adaptive sports had been in her recovery, Kelly was adamant that all injured athletes should have opportunities to compete and access to equipment while on the road to regaining an active lifestyle. Her desire to help led to the launch of the Kelly Brush Foundation (KBF), which has a mission of "empowering those with paralysis to lead engaging and fulfilling lives through sport and recreation." The KBF provides grants to injured athletes who demonstrate financial need for the purchase of equipment for adaptive sports. The foundation also provides grants to ski clubs around the country so they can purchase the necessary safety equipment to prevent ski accidents. On top of these grant programs, the KBF partners with competitive adaptive sports programs to encourage participants to take their talents to the next level.

After rehab, when Kelly returned to Middlebury College in fall 2006, she entered her junior season as an active member of the ski team, training to compete in a monoski on the same slopes she had raced before. She finished out her senior year and raced as an adaptive sports athlete as part of the Middlebury Carnival. After graduating in spring 2008—on time, despite missing a semester due to her injury—she was honored the following year with the highly lauded, rarely bestowed NCAA Inspiration Award.

Ask Kelly Brush about her life today and she shrugs off the challenges. She doesn't set herself apart from others who must learn to adapt in the wake of difficulties or from those who live out their dreams without challenges.

"I don't think my life is any different . . . I'm married, I have a baby, I work in the field that I wanted to work in, I graduated from Middlebury." Her field is nursing and, even between her job and juggling time as a mom and wife, she still has not lost any of her passion for the work of her foundation.

When asked to define kindness, Kelly answers that, though her definition may be cliché, to her, kindness is the time-tested principle of **_doing to others what you would have done unto you_**.

True, many of us have heard the Golden Rule since we were kids, but that doesn't make the cliché any less true or important. Kelly embodies this definition of kindness to its fullest extent. She's also an example of a lesser-known piece of wisdom: The only way to learn to treat others the way you want to be treated is by embracing the experiences, moments, and events that make us who we are . . . no matter how difficult.

We can borrow from Kelly Brush and choose to bring out the tiger in ourselves, getting back out on our own slopes after learning from our difficulties. With that empowerment, we can thereby treat others with the kindness and love we all want and deserve.

Kelly, you are so determined and courageous—a tiger, indeed! Thank you for embodying the Golden Rule and finding a way to do what you love and help so many others in the process. I am so glad that this foundation exists to help others feel the transformative power of being active and free. If you or someone you know has experienced a spinal cord injury and are looking for resources to help you lead an active lifestyle, check out the Kelly Brush Foundation.

Lady Gaga

29

SARAH RYAN

Imagine you're going through a rough time, walking down a dark alley in a strange city, late at night, with not one light on to make you feel a little less desperate and alone. And then imagine how you would feel if you turned a corner and saw a well-lit storefront with a welcome sign and friendly-looking faces inside. They might be strangers, but wouldn't it ease some of your distress to see a smile or two, or just to read a sign that lets you know you won't be turned away?

KINDNESS COSTS NOTHING

In 2011, fourteen-year-old Carrie Shade was thinking along those lines when she decided to create an online movement to encourage kindness and perhaps inspire fellow teens and young adults to identify themselves as being willing to be supportive and helpful of anyone going through a rough time. She thought in particular about mental illness and the level of loneliness and desperation that could lead a person to take their own life.

How powerful can mere kindness be? For Carrie, the answer is that it's more powerful than we often acknowledge. Her feeling is that small acts can have a greater impact than grand gestures.

"I make an effort to smile at people as much as I can, even if I don't know them well or really at all," she says. "People who are struggling are not worth any less. It's important to take care of others—and yourself—whenever necessary. Just showing a little compassion for other people can do wonders."

Fourteen years of age might seem too young to launch a movement that starts small and grows into something much larger, but Carrie had deeply held personal reasons for wanting to try: She had lost her best friend to suicide. Her way of grieving was by learning all she could about mental illness and the causes of suicide. Believing that everyone has the power to make a difference, Carrie established the Against Suicide movement. As a young mental health advocate, she feels uniquely positioned to encourage peers to become informed about how they, too, can help others seriously struggling to seek professional treatment.

Over the years, Carrie has found that creating support for openly talking about mental health issues goes a long way in tackling the social stigma that prevents people from seeking help when they are most in need. "Anyone can be affected by a mental illness, either their own or that of someone they love," she says.

When Carrie made the decision to mount her campaign for mental health as a virtual movement without a brick-and-mortar counterpart, there was no one main reason. She just wanted to put something positive into the world, and she never actually expected it to take off the way it did. For her, Twitter was "like a blank canvas" where she could create and advocate for a cause she believes in.

When many teens and young adults in the community and elsewhere, via social media, chose to be a light in the darkness and to identify themselves as being willing to welcome those looking for support, the movement took off dramatically, eventually winning the Shorty Award for Best in Activism in 2013 and 2014. This award recognized Carrie and her movement for starting social media campaigns such as #ToThoseWhoNeedIt, #StayingClean, and #ProjectLG.

Stories like Sarah's highlight the bravery it takes to ask for help. If someone hasn't told you yet today, please let me be the first and repeat these words to you: You matter, and we need you here, friend. If you or someone you know is struggling with suicidal ideation, please reach out to someone you trust. It might be one of the hardest things you ever do, but it will also be one of the bravest. Check out Against Suicide on Twitter; and please reach out to Crisis Text Hotline to talk to, message, or chat with a trained crisis counselor for 24-7 assistance, or visit the American Foundation for Suicide Prevention to learn more about the signs and symptoms of suicidal ideation.

Lady Gaga

The latter hashtag stands for Project Life Guard, which is an online support group that stemmed from wanting to show compassion online. It aims to help people get through the hardest parts of their lives. To participate, people just write #ProjectLG in their social media bios, which shows others they are there to help.

Against Suicide has also opened a small online merchandise store. The shirts are meant to show the world that people shouldn't be afraid to talk about depression and that all mental illness should be taken seriously.

Through social media platforms like Twitter and Instagram, this movement has reached more than 250,000 people. Over the years, the overall message has stayed the same, but the tone has shifted. Carrie says that it has "transformed from cheesy and cute inspirational quotes . . . to relatable messages that will leave you thinking for a while."

Now in her early twenties, Carrie says, "While it's important to remember that mental illnesses can't simply be cured by spreading positivity, being nice to people can make someone's bad days more bearable."

Putting out the welcome sign, offering a smile, or using a #hashtag that lets other users know you have prioritized their well-being can absolutely make a huge difference. How we treat others on social media, of course, has a corollary in real life. Just showing a little compassion is one of those small acts of great kindness that can change someone else's life—and costs nothing to give.

30

PLANTING SEEDS OF CHANGE
IN SOUTH TEXAS

MARK YOUNG

With more than three hundred thousand people, Corpus Christi is one of the larger cities in Texas, yet it offers few resources or outlets for the LGBTQ+ community—especially its younger members. In general, South Texas isn't necessarily known for its inclusive spaces. In recent times, though, a Corpus Christi youth group is looking to change that.

Youth Network Out Together, also known as YNOT, is a local LGBTQ+ youth group formed to help create the same kind of opportunities to LGBTQ+ youth for connection and belonging that are available to straight youth. With funding from the Elton John AIDS Foundation, YNOT is hosted by the Coastal Bend Wellness Foundation—whose Pride center coordinator, Angie Baker, said she is excited to see a group for young people plant seeds for change and growth in the area.

Angie: "My goal is to make sure that young LGBTQ+ people have access to resources, like health resources, housing, therapy, and more. YNOT currently offers a space for local youth to come and get these resources while having other people to talk to."

YNOT is open to anyone ages thirteen to twenty-four. It offers teens and young adults a safe space to gather, with educational days, games and activities, and community events. In addition to including members in Corpus Christi's annual Pride parades and special events, YNOT created its own LGBTQ+ youth prom—a much anticipated and well-attended event.

Still growing, YNOT has become a kind of family home base that has made a significant difference in the lives of members, often in different ways. Sam Legendre-Davis, twenty-one, a member from the start, likes the social aspects of the group, while Zephyr Reames-Zepeda, twenty-three, joined so he could be more of a role model to younger members and play a role as a community activist. Andy Fergal saw the group as a means of achieving higher visibility for himself and other young people living in the shadows or feeling unsafe about coming out as LGBTQ+.

Here they describe why YNOT matters to each of them.

Sam: *"There aren't a lot of places in Corpus that have safe LGBTQ+ places for people under the age of twenty-one. YNOT has been a great place to meet people and be in an accepting environment."*

Zephyr: *"I joined when I came back to Corpus Christi after college and learned about the group during a trans-alliance meeting, I was never really an activist until my boyfriend committed suicide. He was an activist and opened my eyes to the crisis that LGBTQ+ people face."*

Andy: *"I didn't feel like I saw myself in the community, so I joined this group after hearing about it in a trans support group. This group allows kids to be kids and express themselves how they want to, which they aren't always able to at home or at school."*

Zephyr: *"This group helps young kids see successful older adults who have gone through the struggles of growing up and going to school. And shows them that life can be good and lets me be a role model."*

Whether through Pride events, parades, proms, block parties, or in safe group gatherings, YNOT has already changed the landscape of South Texas—putting down roots in the community and offering shelter, resources, kindness, and strength.

♥

Mark's story sheds light on how important it is to find your community. I believe that everyone should be embraced for who they are, exactly as they are, and I couldn't be more grateful for safe spaces like Youth Network Out Together that encourage acceptance and self-love. To learn more about the YNOT program, visit the Coastal Bend Wellness Foundation or the Elton John AIDS Foundation. If you identify as LGBTQ+ and are in need of a safe, confidential, and judgment-free place to express yourself, contact the Trevor Lifeline today.

Lady Gaga

31

EVIDENCE-
BASED
KINDNESS
IN INDIANA

TAYLOR M. PARKER

There's a saying that if you're not part of the solution, you're part of the problem.

In Indianapolis, an LGBTQ+ youth center called Indiana Youth Group has leaped into the forefront of finding a solution to the growing problem of self-harm for LGBTQ+ youth, who are disproportionately and alarmingly at risk. It's become increasingly clear that the risk is amplified in environments that may be typically discouraging or unwelcoming of LGBTQ+ identities. To improve those environments and stem this rising tide, Indiana Youth Group has developed an evidence-based prevention program that is for at-risk youth across the Midwest.

The cost-free program, called THRIVE: Dare to Be Powerful, focuses on LGBTQ+ youth ages twelve to twenty, providing them with coping skills and encouragement. THRIVE came about after Indiana Youth Group staff discovered that there were no evidence-based suicide prevention programs to use as models that centered on LGBTQ+ youth.

"Evidence-based" means that there is a body of scientific evidence and research being used to guide the practices of a program—as opposed to relying on anecdotal evidence, tradition, intuition, or methods that are unproven or unstudied. In the life-and-death arena of suicide prevention, evidence-based solutions save lives and provide guidelines for the best possible practices and outcomes.

"There were incredible resources, and wonderful work being done," explains the staff at Indiana Youth Group, but the curriculum that was chosen—Coping and Support Training—had the main advantage of being evidence-based, along with its focus on mood management and drug use control.

THRIVE participants have had impressive, measurable benefits, including:

• decreased symptoms of depression

• increased self-esteem

• looking forward to and planning for the future

• developing positive coping skills

• feelings of connectedness to the LGBTQ+ community

• making friends

Kyle Casteel, an Indiana Youth Group alumnus, said that THRIVE is "a very transformational service that doesn't get as much attention. Rates of suicide are so high, and LGBTQ+ young people are especially at risk. This program is something that has been impactful to me personally, so I really see the value in that kind of work . . . When my peer group lost a close friend to suicide, the Indiana Youth Group youth workers went out of their way to make sure I was doing okay. It's that kind of relationship-based work that makes Indiana Youth Group different than other organizations and so important to the community."

Casteel feels that THRIVE is urgently needed for youth in areas of the country that are not as historically and publicly accepting of them. Solutions that work, he believes, are necessary. "LGBTQ+ young people want for so much, especially in our state," Casteel says. No organization or program is perfect, but Indiana Youth Group is offering real solutions. He goes on, "Anyone ready and willing to engage in the hard work it takes to provide our young people with the things they need deserves recognition for that."

Indiana Youth Group's self-harm prevention program is a perfect example of how to assist, encourage, and foster growth in LGBTQ+ youth while promoting safety and community. This program is not standing alone, as Indiana Youth Group has many more programs to keep LGBTQ+ members involved in their communities.

More than anything, Casteel sees the youth-facing staff as a critical component. Their kindness is obvious in all they do. He adds, "They're some of the hardest-working people in their fields, and they are there to help youth get the support they need. Every youth is different, so everyone should know there's no question the folks at Indiana Youth Group won't try to help you work through."

His experience of THRIVE's success is both personal and evidence-based. Problems do have solutions if they are pursued with intention, courage, and a commitment to those they will most impact.

♥

Every LGBTQ+ person deserves to have the resources they need not only to survive, but to thrive, and I commend Taylor for highlighting one of the local resources that takes care of the mental and physical health of our young people. Our team at Born This Way Foundation was so proud to visit the Indiana Youth Group, and it truly is an amazing, evidence-based example of kindness. To learn more about Thrive and how you can help the young people, check out Indiana Youth Group, and if you identify as LGBTQ+ and you're struggling to find resources near you, please visit the LGBT National Help Center.

Lady Gaga

32

TIM SHRIVER **AND** *SPECIAL OLYMPICS*

HANNA ATKINSON

"Let me win, but if I cannot win, let me be brave in the attempt."

These words were spoken by the sister of former US president John F. Kennedy, Eunice Kennedy Shriver, and are known as the oath of Special Olympics—which Eunice founded in honor of their sister, Rosemary, who had a cognitive challenge. Special Olympics, more than any other organization, has dramatically changed how people with disabilities are viewed in this country and around the world.

Not long ago, I had the privilege of interviewing Tim Shriver, Eunice's son, who is chairman of Special Olympics and a special friend of mine. He feels the oath is at the heart of the movement inspired by his aunt Rosemary and founded by his mother. Tim says the oath captures the best values of athletic competition, too: determination, grit, bravery, courage, camaraderie, friendship, and joy. Tim believes the best way to spread those values is by including everyone in the Special Olympics movement.

Q: *Why did you choose to carry on with Special Olympics as your life's work?*

A: It's the most important thing in the world, to include others. It makes me feel like I am contributing something impactful to the world.

Q: *Tell me about a Special Olympics athlete who has had a huge impact on your life and why.*

A: Loretta Claiborne. She taught me that lessons in simplicity and openness are where the truth is. She understands the world with an open heart and simplicity.

From Loretta's biography as a member of the Board of Directors of Special Olympics: Chief Inspiration Officer; Vice Chair, Board of Directors

Claiborne is a world-class runner and gifted motivational speaker who happens to also be a Special Olympics athlete and a person who has an intellectual disability. She has received two honorary doctorate degrees (Quinnipiac University in 1995 and Villanova University in 2003); completed 26 marathons (she fin-ished in the top 100 women of the Boston Marathon with her best time 3:03); received the 1996 ESPY Award–Arthur Ashe Award for Courage; has a 4th degree black belt in karate; is an inductee into the Women in Sports Hall of Fame and into the Special Olympics Pennsylvania Hall of Fame.

She has appeared twice on the Oprah *show, communicates in 4 languages, and is fluent in American Sign Language. In 2000, Walt Disney Productions produced* The Loretta Claiborne Story *about her inspiring life.*

Q: *Tell me about a Special Olympics volunteer who has had a huge impact on your life and why.*

A: My wife, Linda. She started a local Unified Sports team, and all of our five kids played Unified basketball. She wanted to create a program and get our family involved at a local level.

Q: *With the fiftieth anniversary of Special Olympics having just passed, what's new with the movement?*

A: The Inclusion Revolution! We want 100 million people to pledge involvement and commit to inclusive sports, inclusive health, unified schools, and unified leadership. The kickoff was to create a blaze by lighting the eternal flame in Chicago and [to host] a concert.

Q: *Where do you see Special Olympics in ten years?*

A: More Unified Sports teams around the world in their own schools. I would like to see programs that highlight skill, leadership, and joy and for peers to learn from the athletes.

As a member of the Special Olympics family myself, I have enjoyed spending time with Tim on other occasions—in Washington, D.C.; Atlanta, Georgia; and elsewhere. This visit was especially memorable because we had a chance to discuss a book Tim wrote, *Fully Alive: Discovering What Matters Most*.

As I told Tim, it's a flawless book that speaks about changing personal perspective and society. It has encouraged me to look at my greater, God-given purpose.

Q: *Please tell me about your motivation to write your book.*

A: I was learning a lot about Special Olympics athletes and realizing that they have a lot to teach. I felt misunderstood when I told others that. They thought I was doing a nice thing for the athletes. I wanted to write a book to clarify this. I was learning how to live my life—more happy, engaged, and motivated. It was a better way to live—a more loving, compassionate, faithful, and free way to live.

Q: *Who is your target audience for this book?*

A: Anybody interested in trying to find a way to live life with their heart more open.

Q: *Is there anything else you want readers to know about you?*

A: I am grateful to be in this movement, following our athletes and trying to make a difference in the world.

As a Special Olympics athlete, I am grateful for my special friend Tim Shriver, a gentle man who makes time to doodle with an athlete like me at a conference right before he stands up to present a vision of a movement so powerful, it is going to change the world.

If there is only one thing you take away from this interview, I hope you'll remember Tim's point about the way kindness works. At the same time you're volunteering to help bring about positive change for others, you will gain more positive change in your life than you could have ever dreamed. And if you would join with all of us who are eager to be part of the Inclusion Revolution, let the words of our pledge be your guide:

I pledge to look for the lonely, the isolated, the left out, the challenged, and the bullied.

I pledge to overcome the fear of difference and replace it with the power of inclusion.

I #ChooseToInclude.

Hanna, I'm so proud of you for your involvement in Special Olympics and all the work you do to advocate for a more inclusive world! Thank you for profiling Tim Shriver—he is an inspiring man, and he is doing very important work. Our team at the Foundation has had the pleasure of meeting with him many times, and I'm so grateful to have seen firsthand the talent of Special Olympics athletes. This "inclusion revolution" Hanna writes about captures the spirit of a generation that not only accepts differences, but celebrates them. Let's do everything we can to help build a more inclusive world. If you're interested in joining the Special Olympics as an athlete or volunteering for the organization and signing the Inclusion Pledge, check out Special Olympics.

Lady Gaga

33

HOLLABACK
@ HARASSMENT

SOFIA SEARS

I am a 17-year-old female who decided to go to the corner store to get some snacks in the evening. Abruptly this middle-aged male slowed down in his car and asked me if I smoked. I ignored him and continued to walk. I noticed from the corner of my eye that he was following me. He asked me again if I smoked, I said no and continued walking. Then he seemed to get more agitated and told me that I'll have a good time with him. That he wants to see me naked laying in bed with him. When I heard him say that I felt sick to my stomach. I panicked and started to speed walk. He continued to follow me in his car, at this point I was about 50 feet from my house. I didn't want him to know where I lived so I pretended that it wasn't my house and walked the other direction. After 5 minutes of catcalling me he gave up and continued on his way. I ran as fast as I could. Once I got to my house I broke down in tears and had a panic attack. I asked myself—"How could this occur, a 17-year-old female wearing jeans and a long baggy shirt?"

—anonymous post on Hollaback!, July 10, 2019

Being a young woman in the world can be a precarious experience, and finding your footing is anything but simple. Being a young woman inhabiting public space, in particular, is an entirely idiosyncratic, distinctively terrifying experience. Being a person inhabiting public space should not automatically make you the unwitting victim of negative attention and harassment, particularly if you are being attacked because of any facet of your identity.

Hollaback! is an organization working to change this norm and end harassment. For many women, it's so commonplace that we cannot recount the number of times we have been walking alone, or with female friends, and received whistles, crude comments, demeaning remarks, and lewd exposure from random men. No one should ever feel unsafe in their own neighborhood because of how they look or identify, and we will not achieve a welcoming, comfortable environment for everyone until we all recognize this fundamental truth.

Hollaback!'s goal? To ensure that truth.

Hollaback! is an extraordinarily important movement to culturally and systemically de-normalize, and ultimately end, harassment in all its forms. The organization was started by Emily May, a passionate advocate for social change and an accomplished, inspirational disrupter of broken social norms. May sums up Hollaback!'s core beliefs, and the importance of ending the harassment, in one sentence: "We believe free speech is not truly free when it silences other people."

How does her organization work to meet its goals? One way, she says, is via public service announcements on public transportation, by celebrities helping to speak out against harassment, by training businesses how to create harassment-free work environments, and by being clear about what *is* and *isn't* harassment. But what is most valuable, it seems, is sharing individual stories.

The most effective tool so far has been the app of the same name, which helps do exactly that—allow people to instantly share their stories of being harassed. They can post online, noting the specific place and time that the incident occurred. This helps warn nearby users and creates a network of people with similar experiences. Those being harassed can easily post their story, checking options from a list of harassment variations, including:

- Verbal abuse
- Sexual gestures
- Inappropriate touching
- Being followed
- Indecent exposure
- Homophobia

- Transphobia
- Racism
- Sizeism
- Colorism
- Ableism
- Other

One recent post described a situation as follows:

> There are these racist straight white couples incessantly harassing me. This one extremely racist woman would not leave. They were in a car at the bus stop. They were glaring at me and muttering things under their breath for like 25 minutes threatening me.

Emily May explains, "Sharing info on Hollaback! reduces trauma. People stop perceiving it as a horrible thing that happened to them personally." Instead users can understand that the problem is societal. When a thirteen-year-old was harassed for being overweight and was also threatened with sexual taunts, she was able to tag her entry with hashtags like #MeToo, #ListenToWomen, and #EverydaySexismHasGotToStop.

Emily is on a crusade. She recognizes that what is so insidious about street harassment, in particular, is that however innocuous a small comment like "Hello there, beautiful" might seem, for someone who has experienced sexual abuse, it can trigger a form of post-traumatic stress disorder, like "ripping a scab off."

Hollaback! has recently launched campaigns to curb online harassment, which has been an increasingly pervasive problem, especially in this current political climate, with extremist rhetoric and hate crimes sharply on the rise. Emily describes the disturbing trend of female leaders stepping back from having a visible, vocal online presence—all because of extreme online harassment.

Action is needed, and Hollaback! offers guidance. After all, says Emily, "The Internet is just another form of public space," and so applying bystander intervention online is just as effective as in the offline world.

We all deserve to feel comfortable, safe, and welcome and in a world where that is not the reality for far too many people. Hollaback's work is essential and I'm grateful to you for sharing it with us, Sofia. Maya, our executive director, has long boasted about her friend Emily, the movement she built, and the important work that they do, and I'm so glad that you explored it firsthand. To learn more about Emily's mission to end harassment, please check out Hollaback!, and don't forget that your voice matters— as a bystander, as a resource, and as a community member.

Lady Gaga

For any young person who wants to become a member of this social movement against harassment, there are easy, tangible steps that can be taken. Bystander intervention classes are available, offered by Hollaback! and other community resource centers. Empowering yourself with knowledge as to what harassment looks like for different communities is important, as is the choice to reject the kind of behavior too often excused as normal that makes harassment acceptable in our society.

Be brave for yourself and anyone you witness being bullied, berated, threatened, or harassed. The kindness component is basic. It's all about giving a holla and having someone's back and knowing someone else has yours.

34

UGLY FOOD NEEDS *LOVE*

/ ELYSE NOTARIANNI

*E*ntrepreneur magazine defines social entrepreneurship as being "driven not so much by profit as by societal needs that the entrepreneur has identified and is passionate about." A wonderful example of a passion-driven social entrepreneur is Evan Lutz, the CEO of Hungry Harvest, a business he started in his dorm room at the University of Maryland in 2014 after having a radical idea. Evan had been grappling with how he could do something to solve the problem of food waste.

Around 40 percent of all food in the United States goes to waste, and much of that happens before we even buy it. Grocery stores can be incredibly picky when accepting produce from farmers. If a food item does not look like it conventionally should—if it's too big or too small, for example—then it could get thrown away.

At the same time that Evan wanted to fight food waste, he also wanted to address another societal need, which was to provide more fresh produce to individuals living in communities without easy access to healthy foods. Such places are known as *food deserts*.

His radical idea arose from a simple premise:

What if, instead of throwing that unqualified food away, he sold it?

In no time, Evan had set up a small farmers' market–type table on campus and sold his first batch of imperfect produce. He soon used that momentum to create a full-fledged business with five hundred customers, which he increased to almost five thousand after making a deal with Robert Herjavec on the entrepreneur-focused television show *Shark Tank* in January 2016.

Hungry Harvest sells rescued vegetables to subscribers in Washington, D.C.; Virginia; Maryland; Philadelphia; Southern New Jersey; and (soon) Miami. But don't let the word *rescued* scare you. Rescued produce includes fresh fruits and vegetables that are perfectly fine to eat but would otherwise have been thrown away due to aesthetic imperfections or logistical inefficiencies. This could be for something as silly as not fitting into the right-size containers or being an incorrect quantity than what's desired for wholesale purchases. All these exclusions fall under the heading of "ugly food."

Hungry Harvest customers have the option to receive weekly or biweekly mini, full, or super harvests of rescued product. Users can receive all-veggie, all-fruit, or all-organic orders, delivered right to their door. The most popular option is the Mini Standard Harvest (5 to 7.5 pounds of produce for between $15 and $17).

Every week, the Hungry Harvest team sends an e-mail outlining the contents of each box and why the items were rejected—

Eggplant too small to sell in stores?
The HH Team thinks they're cute.

Don't like eggplant anyway?
No problem!

Customers create "Love It" and "Never" lists to identify what they do and do not want to buy. And if the box isn't enough, they can choose add-ons ranging from rescued avocados to baked goods and jams.

This process not only reduces food waste; as a social entrepreneurship, Hungry Harvest finds ways to give back to the community—providing regular produce for food-insecure families and hosting subsidized farmers' markets in neighborhoods without access to fresh food. They've joined with the Baltimore City Public Schools to create Produce in a SNAP—a partnership aimed at promoting healthy eating and fighting hunger in food-insecure neighborhoods.

Evan and his team at Hungry Harvest believe in the model of doing well by doing good. Their business grows and prospers while they also address issues of concern in communities they are helping improve. As they grow as a company, they help others along the way.

The practice of giving love to ugly food and buying rescued produce is being built on an idea whose time is ripe. It supports farmers who now have a chance to make up revenue that otherwise would have been lost. It decreases food waste and helps eliminate the problem of throwing away perfectly good food because of cosmetic issues. It lets families in need buy food at a lower cost. And, if nothing else, it saves you a trip to the grocery store.

We can all do our own part to avoid food waste. As consumers, we have a responsibility to shop more consciously. It's true, as they say, that every dollar you spend is a vote for the world you want to live in.

What's more, the choice to use your power as a consumer to create a kinder, healthier, less wasteful world is not a radical idea at all.

Yet another wonderful reminder to not judge anything or anyone based on how they look—fruits and vegetables included. I love Evan's innovative approach to reducing waste, supporting food-insecure families and community programs, and infusing kindness into your grocery list. Hopefully soon, we'll remove the word *ugly* from the way we talk about people, food, and our communities—I think you're all cute, too! Check out Hungry Harvest, and if you're experiencing food insecurity, please visit Feeding America.

Lady Gaga

35

LUPUSCHICK

MARIA MONGIARDO

The immune system has been described by experts as one of the most miraculous systems in the human body. Every day, through a vast and intricate communication network, its cellular army fights off a constant onslaught of the most vicious foreign invaders that would do us harm. Every now and then, however, the immune system misidentifies a part of itself as a foreign invader and overreacts—causing damage to the very organs and body it's designed to protect. That overreaction is what happens in most autoimmune diseases.

One activist in the study of autoimmune disease is Marisa Zeppieri—a journalist, blogger, and founder of the nonprofit LupusChick. Marisa runs her nonprofit, all while dealing with lupus herself.

As a chronic autoimmune disease that causes your immune system to attack itself, lupus is usually brought on in response to a combination of factors, including hormones, genetics, and the environment. Some symptoms of lupus include fatigue, joint pain, fever, and a butterfly-like rash.

LupusChick's Facebook page is incredibly active, with more than thirty-nine thousand likes and with posts that have reached more than six hundred thousand people—on a monthly basis. Marisa provides advice, posts uplifting quotes, has given five college scholarships to lupus patients, and is a huge inspiration in the autoimmune community.

Marisa's daily reminders run the gamut, from *#LoveYourself* to *#SpreadLupusAwareness*. And she was most gracious in giving Channel Kindness an in-depth Q&A interview.

Q: *Can you talk about the acts of kindness you do every day?*

A: I believe kindness can be shown in a variety of ways, big and small. It starts with a caring and compassionate heart. I've always had the desire to help people, especially those who were struggling in some way. Whether it is helping an elderly person put heavy groceries in his car or rescuing a stray and finding it a loving home, putting yourself out there doesn't require much and the reward is great—you've just made the world a better place in some small way and you loved on someone with no expectation.

Q: *With your diagnosis, do you have time for putting yourself out there?*

A: In my world of LupusChick, my acts of kindness typically revolve around spending time with men and women who are just diagnosed and frightened. Giving them a chance to talk about their fears and ask questions is so cathartic to them, and it brings me great joy to share the experiences I have had knowing they might be able to help someone. We also raise money to help patients—for someone needing money to afford prescription medication, helping a woman find shelter, raising money for a college scholarship program. These are a few examples; the kindest act is just being there. Time is such a precious commodity. To be willing to give up your free time to serve others and expect nothing in return can fill your heart with a joy that is almost unexplainable.

Q: *Why is being kind important to you?*

A: Doing things for others takes you out of your reality, if even for a moment. It causes you to focus less on yourself and your situation and gives you a glimpse into the life and/or situation of another person. Showing kindness can also be life-changing for someone—it may be the first time anyone has treated them in that manner.

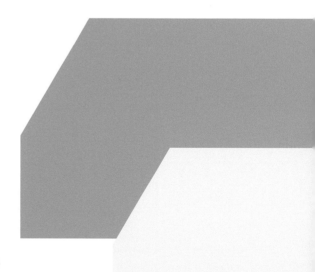

Q: *What's one act of kindness you performed that you believe has affected many people?*

A: I think creating LupusChick has been my "greatest" act of kindness in terms of reach. These are autoimmune patients, their caregivers, spouses, etc. We serve as a safe space for people to ask questions, share experiences, help one another, plus we provide resources, free giveaways and products that help patients, scholarships, and more. It is a great example to show others that . . . taking a leap of faith and creating something that can help someone can have a much greater effect on society than you ever imagined!

Q: *What are ways you suggest to people who want to perform acts of kindness?*

A: Volunteering is always a great way to show people kindness, help others, build relationships . . . the key is being willing to take time out of your day and be willing to give of yourself and expect nothing in return. Whether you take a meal over to someone who is sick, offer to babysit for a single parent who you know could use a break, or visit the elderly who are in a nursing home, the opportunities are endless. You can also look for a need that isn't being met.

Looking for an opportunity to fulfill a need that wasn't being met, in fact, was what Marisa did with LupusChick years ago. Social media and blogging were just getting popular and, as she noted, "It was the perfect time to create a community of support and encouragement when most patients felt alone."

There are so many ways to be proactive when you have an autoimmune disease—including taking precautions to avoid triggering attacks and adopting nutrition plans that help minimize inflammation. Similarly, you can be proactive in pursuing ways to be kind to yourself and to others who are going through the same thing as you.

♥

This disease hits very, very close to home for my family—thank you for profiling Marisa and her work at LupusChick, Maria. LupusChick sounds incredible. Thank you for building a community for lupus patients, caregivers, and loved ones to ask questions, find resources, and connect with one another for support. I love how you said the kindest act is just being there, sitting next to someone, together on the good and bad days. I hope that we each find that, and I encourage you to learn more about chronic illness by checking out LupusChick. Be sure to also check out another organization near and dear to my family, the Lupus Research Alliance; I'm so proud of my father, who sits on the board!

Lady Gaga

LupusChick believes you should

be creative, look past your- self, and keep your eyes open to occasions where you can pour into the life of another.

36

GO *GIRL* GO!

Be Kind.

NICHOLAS McCARDLE

Ask anyone growing up in a community without privilege or much access to opportunity what it's like to be raised without role models—when you don't see anyone successful who even looks or sounds like you. Most will repeat the adage that it's very hard to become something you can't see as possible.

This is as true of rural, impoverished communities as it is of marginalized communities in urban inner cities. Dr. Breanna Nolan, a pediatrician who graduated from the West Virginia University School of Medicine, had her first chance to plant seeds of possibilities for others when she returned to her hometown of Reader, West Virginia. There she implemented an after-school program at Short Line Elementary, the grade school she attended as a child.

The program she created, GoGirlGo!, is an initiative of the Women's Sports Foundation, an organization founded by tennis legend Billie Jean King. Dr. Nolan, a WVU Pediatric Residency Rural Scholar, first learned about this project through her research on various after-school programs she could implement in rural communities.

She was impressed with the statistics supporting its success and liked that the program would be free to those who wished to participate. Designed to focus on girls ranging from ages five to thirteen, GoGirlGo! begins by making sure participants are engaged in thirty minutes of physical activity followed by an additional thirty minutes of health education. Some of these education topics include nutrition, body image, self-esteem, substance abuse, bullying, leadership, diversity, and dealing with difficult emotions. The curriculum is all-encompassing, covering all areas of health, including mental, social, emotional, and physical well-being.

Nothing like that had ever been offered to Dr. Nolan as a little girl. But as a believer that brave new ideas can change lives and improve entire communities, she championed the program—convinced it could make a difference.

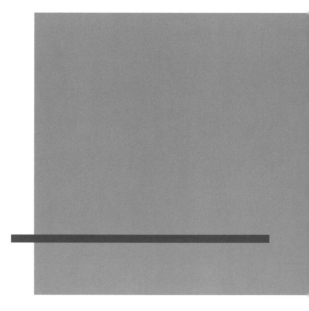

It is no secret that physical activity is a great way to deal with stress, anxiety, and depression. Adding to that principle, Dr. Nolan adapted a form of "walk-and-talk" therapy that combines physical activity with talk therapy, which has been shown to be highly effective. The approach helps promote positivity through the forward motion of walking. By merging exercise with a health education curriculum, Dr. Nolan was excited to create a positive and uplifting environment for her participants. In a safe, supportive environment, she was convinced young girls would be empowered to share their feelings and articulate their dreams and plans.

"I want to give back to the community that gave so much to me as I grew up," Dr. Nolan said. "I think that middle school can be a tough time full of transitions and changes, and I hope that the girls will use these lessons to help them cope and even thrive throughout this integral time of adolescence."

The project is intended to offer girls more opportunities for physical activity outside of competitive sports. Such opportunities were not readily available to Nolan when she was younger, and there were few safe places for children to walk and play outside. Girls may resist the more competitive component of physical activity and miss out on the fun—a pattern Nolan looks to replace. Hopefully an after-school program that encourages girls to have a wonderful time while being active with friends will be of benefit to everyone at school, in their families, and in the town.

Tracy Mason, a teacher at Short Line Elementary, talked about how valuable an effective program could be. "I see girls in my class struggle every day with self-esteem," she noted. "Some of the problems that they encounter are bullying and cliques. Another problem is socioeconomic status. Certain girls feel less than adequate because their opportunities may not be the same as others'." This also applies to materialistic items. Can one after-school program make a difference?

Mason says, "I believe that the GoGirlGo! program has the potential to have a big influence on the youth of our rural community. I think it is important to have a program such as this for girls to have an avenue to express their concerns with their physical and emotional well-being."

Dr. Nolan's initiative gained support from the Wetzel County Board of Education after she gave a presentation detailing her plan to implement GoGirlGo! Her passion and determination to make a difference made quite the impression on the director of secondary and vocational education, Tammy Holbert Wells.

"GoGirlGo! in a remote, rural area like Short Line will impact young girls in ways beyond the mission of the program of increased physical activity," she said. "The young physicians working with these girls will undoubtedly be excellent role models for our students to emulate, and Breanna is one of them."

Wells continued, "How much hope does that give a young girl with a brain on fire and the drive to succeed? Imagine the young lady that has skills and smarts but has never dared to dream of becoming a physician or whatever she wishes? Seeing a physician from her hometown working with others to make a difference just may be the catalyst for her to achieve her dreams."

♥

Nicholas's story highlights the importance of learning how to take care of your mind and body. From meditation to physical activity to learning about nutrition, there are several ways to be kind to yourself, and we encourage you to practice them. My mom loves to do ballet, and I love yoga and gyrotonics—it's important that we all find our own self care practices. Thank you for the important reminder, Nicholas! To learn more about GoGirlGo, we invite you to visit the Women's Sports Foundation.

Lady Gaga

As proactive as GoGirlGo! is, programming alone does not change lives for the better. Rather, it's the people running the programs who make them fly, or not. What they give lasts forever—by being kind and courageous enough to show up and encourage younger individuals to foster their dreams and take the needed steps to make them a reality.

37

STARKVILLE
PROUD

TERRIUS
HARRIS

The story I'm about to report almost didn't happen. It's the story of the planning of a Pride parade in, of all places, Starkville, Mississippi.

Pride! It's a time where millions of LGBTQ+ individuals around the world are able to fully express and celebrate who they are. A time when, no matter your differences, there is a home for everyone. Pride parades in particular are known for their extravagant displays of love of all kinds and a unique feeling of joy for all. Said parades are usually held in more liberal cities, such as New York City; Washington, D.C.; or Atlanta.

And yet, in what was potentially a monumental step forward, Starkville—which is commonly known as a small, conservative city in a conservative state—had an opportunity to join the ranks of the aforementioned cities.

This is a story where discrimination and exclusion were poised to stop a major success. However, this is also a story about how the powers of courage and kindness combined to become a force greater than the sum of those parts.

It begins in late 2017, when twenty-two-year-old Starkville Pride Director and Founder Bailey McDaniel had a vision in which Starkville would not only hold its first Pride parade ever but also the largest parade of any kind in its city's history.

But, in a firm rebuke, the Starkville Board of Aldermen voted upon and denied the request to hold the parade. For a moment, it appeared there was no recourse. Refusing to give up, the Starkville Pride leaders opted to file a lawsuit against the city based on their alleged discriminatory decision. After the filing of this lawsuit, the board again voted to bring the event back into consideration, and after a 3–3 tie, Starkville Mayor Lynn Spruill cast the tie-breaking vote—which was the turning point in favor of Starkville Pride. Planning could move forward to bring Bailey's vision for the Pride parade to life.

On the morning of March 24, 2018, the Pride leaders nervously wondered how many participants would actually show and whether or not there would be threats along the route. But at the appointed hour, as Bailey arrived with other Pride leaders, they saw no reason to worry: An estimated three thousand people had shown up to be part of the parade! It was their first-ever LGBTQ+ parade, of course, and the largest parade of any kind in the city's history.

People, no matter if they were straight, gay, bisexual, transgender, black, or white, joined together to show their support for the community they love. Marching side by side, step by step, thousands rejoiced. The excitement was contagious. People have marched in Mississippi before to bring about change, and this Pride parade was also an important step in the state's history.

An event of celebration and representation of the city's value for its diverse populations, the day changed Starkville forever. A true light in the dark, the story to be told does not need to focus on its beginning, but instead on its happy ending. The conclusion has inspired countless young people to know that they, too, can make a change. For a community of people, it reaffirmed that not only do they belong in Starkville—they are welcomed with open arms.

The Starkville Pride Parade was an event that changed the face of Starkville and, with any luck, inspired other small rural LGBTQ+ leaders to push forward, just as Bailey McDaniel did.

Although it had a rough beginning, hopefully this uplifting story has left the world a better place and caught the attention of others wishing to make change and, giving them hope, just like a rainbow after a terrible storm.

Change requires vision for a better day and not giving up hope when all looks unfair and mean. Change requires courage, like that of a twenty-two-year-old Pride parade organizer and the mayor of a small Mississippi town who was willing to cast a tie-breaking vote in favor of fairness and inclusion. Most of all, it takes a village—one composed of all those who marched in pride for themselves and one another.

When Starkville—and other places like it—win at opening arms and hearts to all members of our community, we all win.

Love always wins, and Terrius' story is proof of that. The LGBTQ+ community should be respected and embraced, and if you identify as LGBTQ+, know I wholeheartedly celebrate you just the way you are. You matter. You are important. And I promise you, you are loved. If your community doesn't celebrate Pride, I encourage you to safely start your own movement. For resources on building a LGBTQ+ inclusive community, visit Center Link or GLSEN, and if you identify as LGBTQ+, check out TrevorSpace, an online affirming community for LGBTQ young people.

Lady Gaga

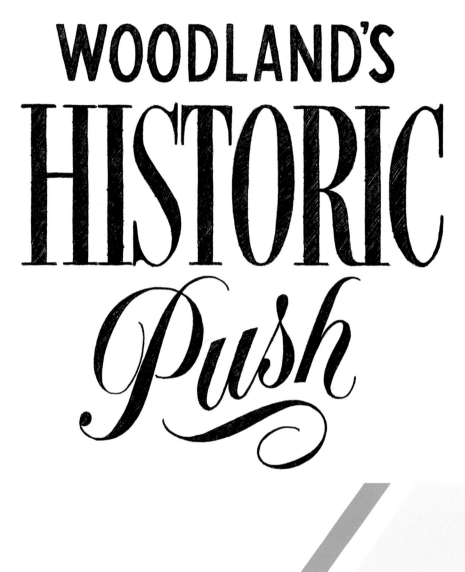

38

WOODLAND'S HISTORIC *Push*

JUAN
ACOSTA

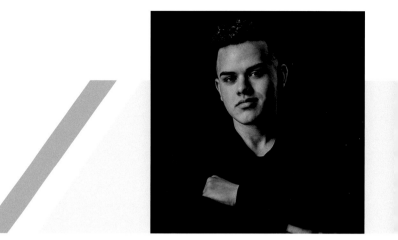

As a young person growing up in Woodland, California—a mid-size city of fifty-five thousand people or so, not far from the state capital of Sacramento and driving distance to San Francisco—I always felt that when it came to being *out*, my hometown was still stuck in the past, in a time of intolerance and exclusion.

Just over twenty years ago, in 1998, Woodland's city council voted down a filing that would have allowed a gay Pride celebration to be held within our city limits. By the summer of 2018, I hoped there would be a much different prevailing attitude. When I arrived at City Hall on the evening of Tuesday, June 19, I tried to reassure myself that there would be no last-minute detractors and that local leaders would agree it was time to celebrate a historical and long-overdue moment. A moment I knew would bring happiness but, furthermore, would provide a message of empowerment to so many people in our community.

From the instant I looked around at the smiling faces of all present, I knew history was going to be made in Woodland, California, as the city proclaimed June the official LGBTQ+ Pride Month. I was one of many who had helped draft the proclamation, in addition to fellow community member Marie Perea, who pushed for the resolution to pass.

Then-Mayor Pro Tempore Xóchitl Rodriguez stated that the Pride Month proclamation was an essential step toward empowering the LGBTQ+ community for their contributions to the city. She began,

"We want to ensure that all community members feel welcomed regardless of sexual orientation or gender identity."

The proclamation seemed to do exactly that—fulfill and send across a message of empowerment and welcome to many members of the community. One of them was Favio Tello, twenty-four, who identifies as queer.

Favio spoke in support of the proclamation during the public comment session and shared his excitement after the proclamation passed. Eager to be a part of such a historic and meaningful moment, he stepped forward to solemnly say,

"My closeted self would have loved to see this visibility brought forth for the LGBTQ community." **Then, more boldly and with a proud smile, he added, "The queers are here, darling, and we are never going to back down!"**

City council member Angel Barajas shared that he believes the proclamation is an acknowledgment. In his words, it is a message "that city leaders not only proclaim that LGBTQ+ members have always been an integral part of our community, but the need of equitable treatment, education, and acceptance must continue for everyone."

This proclamation will remain in the city's history books forever, but the impact that this change has is unbounded.

Juan, what a beautiful story and an incredible gift you've given your community, and Favia, yassss. Last year at WorldPride, I shared my own story about struggling to be accepted, not to compare but as a reminder that we need to love and be proud of who are (and do the same for others). Everyone should be celebrated, the world needs more love and pride, and I'm so grateful you brought it to Woodland and embody it every day. To read more about the history of Pride and find resources on how to support your community, please check out the Human Rights Campaign.

Lady Gaga

The message of embracement for a community longing for acceptance and inclusion was crucial—a true testament that a simple message of kindness and belonging can not only welcome many but also uplift those who feel alone, forgotten, and abandoned.

As much as I had longed for this history-making moment to have taken place earlier, the fact that I was able to help and be a part of a historic moment, to help out my LGBTQ+ brothers and sisters, is one of the greatest experiences to have happened in my life. Seeing people raise their Pride flags, cry, and smile in triumph, love, and excitement is something that will remain with me forever.

39

LOVING BETTER

IN NEW YORK

BROOKE A. GOLDMAN

If you are a busy New Yorker who, by chance, was dashing off to work or to a social engagement in the middle of a freezing-cold February not long ago, and you happened to pass by the corner of Bowery and Prince Street in Lower Manhattan, you might have spotted an unfamiliar sight: a romantic-looking pop-up called Love Better, seemingly devoted to the Valentine's Day season and gift-giving.

If that had been your guess as to the pop-up's purpose, you only would have been half right. Of course, from the outside, if you were just sneaking a peek through the large storefront's windows, Love Better—lined with pink walls, decorated in hearts and balloons galore—did look like any other Valentine's Day store. But the moment you stepped inside, you would have discovered that the pop-up was much more than a gift shop. By the time you walked out, you might well have learned vital, even life-saving, knowledge about the differences between healthy, loving relationships and unhealthy, potentially abusive ones.

The pop-up was one of many installations, public awareness campaigns, educational programs, and media outreach efforts undertaken by the **One Love Foundation**, which seeks to promote safe and loving relationships among young people. **While love, in all its splendor and/or heartbreak, is the most important thing in most of our lives, we are never really taught how to love.** We aren't given classes in how to know if we are being loved better, how to identify the warning signs of relationship or dating violence, how to avoid abuse before it begins, or what to do and how to seek help when we have begun an involvement in which the only emotion we feel is negativity.

In the beginning, little else can feel as thrilling as the exhilaration of falling in love or the excitement of a new attraction, crush, or flirtation. And as feelings deepen, it's so flattering to hear the words of being loved and adored and desired. When intimacy occurs, both emotional and physical, the tightening of the bonds between the two of you can lead to a love that is real, caring, and respectful.

Sometimes, though, what masquerades as good love turns into something that is not healthy and can become harmful, dangerous, or much worse. At first, the signs of an abusive relationship may go unnoticed or ignored. Maybe it was something as small as a critical or controlling comment meant to guilt or manipulate—what you wear, what you can and can't post, what music you like, where you go, who you choose to have as close friends or confidantes. Likewise, physical threats, lashing out in temper, or isolating you from family and others may seem minor in the beginning. Maybe there was a push or a slap, maybe a punch combined with yelling and demeaning words. Maybe there was behavior that could have been seen as stalking or invading space but which could also be interpreted as mere overzealousness.

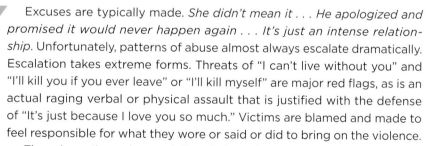

Brooke's story discusses the importance of healthy relationships, something we cannot talk about enough. Love should be a transformational force of good that guides communities every day, you're right. In every relationship you have, you deserve to feel safe, respected, and cared for. You deserve to feel loved. I am both heartbroken by the need for the work of One Love and grateful for the important conversations they've sparked. If you are or a friend is struggling with an abusive relationship, I encourage you to visit Love Is Respect to message, talk to, or text a trained counselor today, and to take an escalation workshop, check out One Love Foundation.

Lady Gaga

Excuses are typically made. *She didn't mean it . . . He apologized and promised it would never happen again . . . It's just an intense relationship.* Unfortunately, patterns of abuse almost always escalate dramatically. Escalation takes extreme forms. Threats of "I can't live without you" and "I'll kill you if you ever leave" or "I'll kill myself" are major red flags, as is an actual raging verbal or physical assault that is justified with the defense of "It's just because I love you so much." Victims are blamed and made to feel responsible for what they wore or said or did to bring on the violence.

There is no time when a victim of abuse is more at risk of danger than when there has been an effort to leave the relationship. Awareness and the courage to turn to advocates for help are absolutely essential. Relationship violence affects every socioeconomic sector and every age group. One in three females and one in four males will, at some time in their lives, experience some form of domestic abuse—what's been described as "the quiet crime," because it takes place behind closed doors.

In May 2010, Yeardley Love, a twenty-two-year-old senior, top student, and lacrosse star at the University of Virginia, was found in her dorm room, beaten to death by her ex-boyfriend. Known for her many talents and as a constant source of kindness, Yeardley was three weeks shy of graduation. On the playing field, she happily wore a number one on her jersey. All of her friends and family said that "to know her was to love her." The tragic irony, as the One Love Foundation put it, is that her life was ended by the very person who insisted he *loved* her.

The shock of her daughter's death still haunts her mother, Sharon, who, together with Yeardley's sister, Lexie, established the One Love Foundation. The organization empowers young people with knowledge about how to #LoveBetter. Sharon has talked about her own lack of awareness, saying, "I didn't know then what I know now, that relationship abuse is a public health epidemic and that young women in Yeardley's age group are at three times greater risk than any other demographic." Sharon and Lexie believe that if more of the young people and others in Yeardley's life had been able to see the warning signs, they would have been able to intervene—and she would still be alive today.

Working in virtual and real classrooms around the country, using such materials as a film entitled *Escalation* about a fictional young couple that exemplifies the perils of relationship violence, One Love has reached millions of viewers and has impacted more than half a million individuals in person. The Valentine's Day pop-up in New York was another creative outreach effort to educate in a new and compelling way.

After all, it's still uncommon to have conversations about the differences between healthy and unhealthy relationships. In reality, although V-Day is supposed to be about romance and a celebration of loving relationships, its value seems more to do with it being a booming, multimillion-dollar industry. The pop-up store idea answered the pressing question of how to shine a light on the true meaning of love, when, for most marketers around the world, it has long been all about business.

Cameron Kinker, the foundation's engagement coordinator, explains, "We envisioned this pop-up as a place where people would come in and expect to buy a Valentine's Day gift, but instead, they see all of these items that have signs of unhealthy behaviors. We want to call attention to a lot of the unhealthy behaviors normalized in our relationships today."

The first thing you would notice walking in might be the selection of gifts offered. For instance, there was a teddy bear that said, "Shut up . . . Wait, I'm sorry. That wasn't the real me," or a chocolate box with the words, "I love you, but maybe you should watch your weight." Both are examples of unhealthy communication meant to control and manipulate. Both compel customers to look at conversations that involve listening, caring, and respecting each other. Those are the true gifts that come from learning how to #LoveBetter.

The One Love Foundation, named for a young woman whose last name was Love, strives to show us that being kind to one another—in relationships, at schools, on our city streets, and in our world—is undeniably possible to achieve. Wherever the message surfaces—at a pop-up Valentine's Day–themed store in New York City and whenever or wherever else—we are reminded that

love should be a transformational force of good that guides communities every day.

We all deserve to #LoveBetter.

4 0

BEYOND

THE PAGES

TYRAH MAJORS

Once upon a time, there was a little girl who had her own dreams of who she wanted to be when she grew up. Not a princess, as some others might dream. Not an astronaut, a veterinarian, nor a teacher. All of those are fine dreams, of course! But this little girl—let's call her Tyrah—dreamed of being an author one day. She loved to make up stories, then write them down, and she read all the time.

The only problem with almost all the storybooks Tyrah read was that mostly all the characters were white or nonhuman. As an African American girl, she wished that the pictures showed children and adults who looked like her.

Tyrah—okay, you guessed it, that's me—slowly let go of her dream of becoming an author. Why? For many of us, dreams evolve and change as we grow up, and we don't always listen to that voice inside of us saying we can do and be whatever we put our energies toward. For me, life became more demanding, and other goals took precedence.

Then, shortly after my great-grandma passed away in late 2014, instead of dreaming about being an author, I actually sat down to write and illustrate a children's book based on my personal experiences with her. *Grammy and Me* captures a day in the life of a loving relationship between a grandparent and a grandchild, while celebrating the magic and wisdom shared from one generation to the next and the importance of family.

We forget sometimes that our first and often most lasting influences come from the family members who teach us about the world, history, and self-awareness. My hope in telling this story is to remind readers of that magic. Too often, as I look around in public places, I see kids with their parents but without much interaction. The little ones often have some sort of electronic device in hand, and the parents are usually having their own conversations.

Technology is part of our lives, for sure, but there is no replacement for talking to and truly interacting with your children during their early years. Those interactions play a vital role in making sure kids gain the guidance to thrive and live their lives positively. My great-grandmother kept the two of us busy with shopping, dining, and cooking, all while sharing an education's worth of life lessons with me.

Grammy and Me, the story of an African American little girl and her great-grandma, is also intended to promote diversity in children's literature. A 2015 statistics states that 85.8 percent of children's books are about white or nonhuman characters—clearly this is not an accurate depiction of the world. Remembering my wish as a child, I really believe we need more diverse books, so that kids of color can grow up seeing themselves represented in the stories they read.

The first time I heard a young reader say, "Oh, she has the same hair as me!" while pointing to my book was priceless.

More than anything, writing a book and fulfilling a dream that had fallen by the wayside was the kindest thing I could have done for myself—a big kick in the pants to remind me, and others who I'd love to inspire, that whenever self-doubt creeps in, change your mindset. Believe me, the self-doubt I had was brutal. *Nobody hired me to write a kids' book. What was I thinking? Who's going to buy it? How can my illustrations compete with the pros?* And so on.

Luckily, I pushed through and ignored the self-doubt. Before long, I was an author—my dream—with a published book I was selling and changing how children in my community get to see themselves represented on the page.

Whenever self-doubt surfaces, it might help to take a look at someone in your family (like my grammy) or someone you admire and remember all the odds they had to overcome. So can you!

Bottom line, I hoped my dream would come true and that my writing would help make a change; to portray things that most children's books don't, all pertaining to kindness, which flows throughout the pages. One fellow Channel Kindness reporter once said, "There's kindness everywhere, you just have to know where to look!"

Kindness really can be found anywhere, even on the shelves of the library and in the pages of a story about a woman gone from our midst who wanted us all to dream of a kinder world beyond mine.

♥

Thank you, Tyrah, for pushing through, overcoming your self-doubt, and writing a beautiful book about your relationship with your grandma. I am fortunate enough to have two grandmas alive today, and I am so grateful for my special relationship with each of them. Seeing ourselves represented in the pages of a book—written by us, told by characters that look like each of us, and with experiences that mirror ours—is vital for young minds. Thank you for not just searching for that story, but for creating it when you couldn't find it. For young people of color who are reading this and want to write more, please check out Writers of Color, or for more resources and a community, check out People of Color in Publishing.

Lady Gaga

41
MORE THAN JUST A BLANKET
THERESA STIER

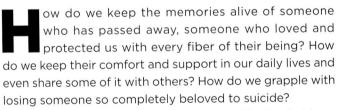

How do we keep the memories alive of someone who has passed away, someone who loved and protected us with every fiber of their being? How do we keep their comfort and support in our daily lives and even share some of it with others? How do we grapple with losing someone so completely beloved to suicide?

Those aren't easy questions to answer. That's what happened to three sisters—Angela, Christina, and Mia Varney—whose mother, Annie, died by suicide at a young age after struggling with debilitating depression.

The heartbroken daughters comforted one another in their grief, and then, together, came up with a way to keep their mom's memory alive: by making Annie's Kindness Blankets. The idea was a "pay-it-forward kindness campaign" created by them, three young girls "dedicated to #BeTheVoice and help stop the stigma around depression and suicide." Their purpose was to create blankets as everlasting hugs for anyone in need, to let others know they were never alone.

Taking turns telling their story, they recalled how the idea came about:

"Whenever we were sad or having a difficult day, or even when we were so happy, a hug from our mom would instantly improve our day. Her hug was warm, generous, and heartfelt. We decided blankets were the best way to reproduce the essence of a hug from her. It made sense to us, to pass along as many of these hugs as possible to people all over. A hug that doesn't judge, doesn't let go. It is comfort or joy when you need it. All made with unconditional love."

We all need hugs in life, especially through the hard, bleaker passages. What better way to do that than wrapping yourself in a blanket when no one is around? You might wonder how these blankets provide kindness or how they're any different from a blanket you could get at a store. These blankets are unique because they've been created by the daughters of Annie—along with help from the girls' aunt, cousin, and community—each of whom has sewn a message of kindness of heart into the blanket, each of whom feels your pain and your loss and is there for you.

Annie's daughters understand the journey of grief:

"People deal with the loss of a loved one differently from one another. Some deny, some cry until they are numb, some visit the place of burial, some silently and emotionally shut down. This was something so tragic and so horrible that happened to our family, we needed a ray of light to help heal our hearts. When our mom passed, we were lost—we were living in a haze. Nothing made sense and the world seemed chaotic. We needed something to calm our souls. To give to others to let them know that they are never alone. We wanted others to remember that there are kind people in this world who truly care. This is what we chose to do, to help keep peace in our broken hearts."

Within a year, the Varney sisters had given out well over 1,100 blankets, and had more than sixty people helping to create these blankets—adding to the warmth and healing power of blankets that bring people together from the moment they are made to the moment they are delivered. How amazing is that?

♥

What a beautiful way to keep Annie's memory alive and to share warmth and connection with so many others. I believe that the best type of kindness is the one that inspires kindness in others—and by sharing the blankets, giving that warm hug when someone feels alone, the three of you are catalysts for kindness. You are making a huge difference and realizing Annie's hope that people know that they are never alone. If you want to help make blankets or if you need a blanket (as we all do sometimes), please check out Annie's Kindness Blankets.

Lady Gaga

The ability to keep Annie's memory alive is profoundly demonstrated in this pay-it-forward campaign. And, as they describe it, the sisters feel her presence daily, connecting them to others who are doing healing work:

"Whenever we reach out and ask for help, we can't explain the amount of responses we get in return. We believe that the passing of our mom has directly affected thousands of lives. We believe that she has helped us to help others understand that you may be the most incredible, beautiful, kindest soul on this planet and have so many love you, and still feel so alone inside. She, along with our community, has helped us change the stigma of depression, mental illness, and suicide. They have teamed up with us in so many ways to ensure others know that they are never alone. They have been a lifeline to us."

These girls are not only remembering their mother in such a beautiful way; they are helping others in the process. And that, they believe, is exactly what Annie would have had them do—to #BeTheVoice of kindness.

42

PARTIES WITH

PURPOSE

RILEY GANTT

Nothing happens by accident—especially when it comes to connecting to someone who you just have to feel is in your life for a reason.

It has always felt absurd to me (in a good way) when two people miss a connection one time and make it another. It's like the universe saying, *Hey, you missed something special!*

That's what happened with me and Lulu. There were so many opportunities for us to connect back in the days when my mom owned an art studio called Tinker. Hundreds of people passed through those doors, some of whom we got to know pretty well. One of these people was Lisa Cerone, mom of Lulu and Jasper. Though my mom and Lisa were friendly, I am not entirely sure that I ever actually talked to Lulu or her mom because I was usually the active girl running around the store "helping" my mom. After Tinker closed, for the most part that seemingly would have been the end of crossing paths with most of the store's patrons.

Imagine my surprise a few years later when I was invited to speak at an empathy and leadership camp called My Name My Story where our paths would cross yet again. On the list of names of presenters there was mine—Riley Gantt, founder of Rainbow Pack, a nonprofit that delivers backpacks full of homework and art supplies to kids who don't have those basics at home. On the list was also what I should have spotted as another familiar name, Lulu Cerone, even though I didn't make the connection.

Two years older than I am, with blunt black bangs and an air of coolness about her, Lulu founded a nonprofit called LemonAID Warriors (the topic of her presentation). That, too, should have gotten my attention, because I hadn't met many other kids like me, who ran nonprofit organizations. Thankfully, my mom was there with me and so was Lulu's mom.

Wouldn't you know it? Our moms immediately recognized each other. Sure enough, this girl was Lulu from Tinker.

We all ended up reconnecting, and ever since, I have looked up to her.

We joke that I am always one step behind Lulu, but not in a bad way. When it comes to awards, speaking engagements, conferences, and so forth, Lulu always seems to do everything one year before I do. A role model, she is confident, charismatic, and passionate, someone who is eager to offer advice on running charities while still in middle school and high school.

When Lulu mentioned she was writing a book, I was overjoyed.

"It's going to be good," I burst out. "Better than good. It will be . . . utterly amazing!"

When she asked if she could feature me in the book, that blew my mind. Then again, I was thrilled to contribute what I'd learned from being a kid wanting to create change and how to go about finding resources. What an honor to do so.

Lulu's book, *PhilanthroParties!*, is a recipe for spreading kindness through action—something the world really needs right now. The description alone is powerful:

Why just party when you can party with a purpose? Eighteen-year-old Lulu Cerone shows young people how to bring social activism into their daily lives—and have fun while doing it—with this colorful DIY party planning guide perfect for every socially conscious kid!

Her impulse for writing the book is clear: to motivate young people to get involved and feel the empowerment that comes from that. With so much practical advice, the process comes across as fun and easy. Lulu teaches readers how to throw as many as thirty-six different parties, each inspired by a personal experience that comes with a memorable story and each benefiting a different cause. One of her favorite chapters (there are a few) is about throwing an Ugly Food Feast. Lulu described it as "a dinner party where the meal is made out of food that would typically be wasted. There's a recipe for veggie burgers made out of juice pulp, salad made from imperfect-looking vegetables that grocery stores would normally throw out, and banana bread made from brown bananas. It sends a powerful message about food waste and gets the conversation started."

Just as young people have the capacity to use social media to get attendees to turn out for social events, learning to use our networks for causes we care about and for book launches is equally important. At Lulu's first big book party, hosted by a local bookstore, they sold out of the book, which, Lulu told me, "The manager said has never happened at an author event in their store's history!"

The message of the book offers a huge takeaway from the author:

"Anybody, regardless of their age, can positively impact our world. A simple message, but it's so profoundly important."

Since I had a friend so close to my age who started her own charity when she was very young, I had to ask Lulu what got her started and what kept her going all these years.

The story she told me wasn't of an overly ambitious ten-year-old with dreams of running a nonprofit. She just had always run lemonade stands to raise money for local causes. "It was just a fun thing that I did with my friends, and the fact that we were helping people made it even cooler."

Then came a major event: the 2010 earthquake that struck Haiti. It inspired Lulu's first emotional response to a global issue. "I remember seeing images of the damage and crying. I wanted to help in any way that I could, so I stuck with what I knew best and organized a lemonade stand competition between the boys and girls in my class. We ended up raising $4,000 in two weeks, and it was an incredible, empowering experience." Afterward, Lulu wanted to continue raising money for important causes, all while having fun. "So I established LemonAID Warriors to make things more official." The message that young people can have a powerful and positive impact on the world is why she has continued working on LemonAID Warriors.

The theme of combining philanthropy with fun and hanging out with friends was a key motivation for writing her book—to encourage teens who can't seem to find time for community service not to look at it as an obligation but rather as an opportunity to make a difference together. Her point? Adding "social action to social lives."

Doing the work of running an organization still takes time, as I've learned. I was curious as to how raising money for meaningful causes had impacted Lulu.

She thought about it and said, "It's had such a massive impact on me! I think, overall, it's made me a kinder, more aware person. I've been much more conscious of the needs surrounding me since getting involved when I was young, both in my own community and in the world at large." In fact, all of that shaped her goals for the future. "Now that I'm entering my freshman year of college, I'm considering pursuing international politics, which is definitely due to my experiences growing up. Also, I definitely think that practicing generosity at a young age instilled a tendency within me to be kind to others and help out whenever I can. One of the main reasons why LemonAID Warriors seeks to work with youth is because I truly believe that if you start giving back while you're young, you're much more likely to continue spreading kindness and having a greater awareness as you grow older—and hopefully for the rest of your life."

As my role model, Lulu cleared something up for me about the cynics out there who don't really understand social activism. She confessed that, once she became a senior in high school, a lot of people suggested that the only reason she was running a charity and publishing a book was to get into a good college. "I've heard a lot of snarky comments about that, from both peers and adults alike. It's definitely a little hurtful, because it assumes that my intentions with LemonAID Warriors are self-serving, which is certainly not the case." Lulu sighed. She quickly added, "I know that often those comments, especially when they come from people my age, are out of insecurity, which usually peaks during college application season. I've sort of learned to brush them off, because I know that I do what I do out of a passion to help others, and at the end of the day, that's all that really matters."

There was just one more big question I had to ask my friend and role model who had accomplished so much at an early age: "*What's next?*"

She told me about her plans for college at Columbia University and how excited she is to focus on all that she would be learning. With her vice president taking over the day-to-day running of LemonAID Warriors, she would still be involved, but not so intensively. No doubt, she emphasized, "Activism will definitely play a huge role in my college life, but I'm really looking forward to this next chapter of exploration."

The more I thought about how the universe connected me to Lulu, the more grateful I felt for the kindness champions in my life.

Kindness is a connecting force, I believe, that creates bonds between people with shared concerns.

One of the suggestions in Lulu's book is actually to throw a party that's not about raising money but simply about raising kindness.

Why not?

Kindness costs nothing, changes the world, empowers those who practice it and, in the end, can never, ever be stopped.

♥

Riley, you and Lulu sound like people I'd want to hang out with—parties and do good'ing? Yes, please. At Born This Way Foundation we always say that it's not enough to just talk about kindness, you have to take an action in service to someone else without the expectation of anything in return. You have to actually be kind, not just talking about being kind and what a fun way to do exactly that—PhilanthroParties! You should meet Taylor Parker from Indiana, they'd think this was rad too. To find out more about the people partying with a purpose, search the hashtag #philanthroparties and take that inspiration to plan your own!

Lady Gaga

43

FINDING THE *Spark*

AMY SUN

The decision to become a volunteer for any worthy endeavor is one I heartily encourage everyone to consider, regardless of whatever capacities you think you may have. You may think that it's something to do for others, but I also believe that what you receive back from your efforts will be of equal or greater measure. That was the lesson I learned recently, when I began volunteering at Erie Neighborhood House for a program in Chicago that provides tutoring primarily for low-income communities.

Their Tutoring to Educate for Aims and Motivation (TEAM) program provides weekly tutoring and mentorship for teens in seventh to twelfth grades, who are largely first-generation and want to go to college. Since 1998, 97 percent of their TEAM students have moved on to college, with TEAM providing scholarships as well as comprehensive workshops on the financial aid application process.

When I met my first student, a ninth grader, I introduced myself. "Hello. My name is Amy Sun, and I'm going to be your tutor." I could tell pretty quickly that she was having trouble finding the motivation to study. The more I tried to make suggestions, the more I saw a need to find the right spark to light in her.

One day, the site coordinator decided to pass out notebooks as prizes for finishing the homework set. Interestingly enough, my student really perked up when she heard that, and I noticed it was a great motivator to get through all her worksheets. After realizing that the students could be inspired by the right incentives, I decided to write to a local college, the University of Chicago, asking for a donation of anything college-related to help students stay focused.

Right away, they sent her a T-shirt, which both excited and motivated her going forward.

After the success with the university, I decided to get other colleges on board with donations for underprivileged kids.

/ All of a sudden, the spark was lit in me.

Without a lot of time to contact a long list of colleges, I had the idea to write a code in Google Apps Script. This way, I could send requests via automated e-mails to 1,600 colleges across the nation, including Swarthmore College, Regent College, and the University of California Irvine.

Like an avalanche, I began receiving dozens of packages a day containing T-shirts, pamphlets, pens, notebooks, and even toothbrushes, totaling up to more than three thousand items—enough to expand our number of beneficiaries.

With the help of Erie Neighborhood House, we got in contact with a classroom of highly motivated students. During one afternoon, my sister and I donated all the items we had collected to the students. Watching their reaction to the gifts was wonderful, as was seeing them eagerly discussing the college pamphlets as they learned more about potential opportunities for higher education. The buzz spread.

Later that week, the assistant director of Erie's foundation, Maria Munoz, wrote to me. "Thank you so much for coming and donating, Amy! Kids have been wearing the college shirts all this week."

Looking to light a spark in a student lit a spark in me.

In the process, I was able to put my professional skills to use and multiply the results of my efforts. As I learned, a little incentive can go a long way in motivating a student to do the work that will pave their way to college and beyond. There is nothing more rewarding to me than the satisfaction that comes from knowing I made an impact on others' lives in order to help them in a lasting, meaningful way.

♥

In her story, Amy writes about the importance of education, and I share her excitement in encouraging students to reach their full potential. Young people will rise to the expectations we set for them; I know I did, and I'm so grateful to my parents for believing in me. If you live in Chicago, check out Erie Neighborhood House, and to help young students achieve success in school, consider becoming involved in a mentorship program such as Big Brothers Big Sisters or iMentor.

Lady Gaga

44

KIND WORDS CHANGE MINDS, HEARTS, AND, SOMETIMES, SOCIETY

CONNOR LONG

My name is Connor Long, and as I write these words, I have to say that it is much easier for me to *act* with kindness than to write about it. As a young person with Down syndrome, I am challenged by having great trouble clearly expressing the most typical thoughts, emotions, dreams, goals, and desires. So, when I venture forth on writing projects, I often enlist someone who can help structure my thoughts and clarify my words until I know that what goes down on paper reflects the essence of what I have to say.

As an everyday person, throughout my activities I can easily choose to be kind, to speak kindly, to listen kindly, and to simply be present with someone in need of kindness. It is always an option in front of me.

But as an advocate for people with differing abilities (*dif-abilities*), sometimes I have to actually tell people *why* kindness is important in our lives and in our laws. As if it weren't plain enough:

Kindness ripples,
as does unkindness.

These days, when it is often too hard to find kindness in our politics, let us be sure to find kindness, fairness, and equity in our own words, both public and private.

For example, while *mental retardation* was once a clinically appropriate and useful term, its slang shorthand—*retard*—has become a common and willfully demeaning and hurtful slur that invites taunting, stigma, and stereotype. It invites bullying from the heartless and slammed doors from the mindless. It undermines the simple human need and right to be treated with respect and dignity.

So, yes, we advocates consider the term a stinging label that is outdated, stigmatizing, and needs to go away. But not everyone is embracing the shift. Critics say that changing the word is an act of "political correctness" rather than any substantive change.

Peter V. Berns, CEO of nonprofit The Arc of the United States, says it best: "We understand that language plays a crucial role in how people with intellectual disabilities are perceived and treated in society. Changing how we talk about people with disabilities is a critical step in promoting and protecting their basic civil and human rights."

The Arc, which promotes and protects the rights of people with intellectual and developmental disabilities, has been advocating the use of the term *intellectual disability*. It is the reasonable position of The Arc that "The only 'R-word' that should be used when referring to people with intellectual and developmental disabilities is *respect*."

I completely agree.

So my message on how to channel kindness is to ask you to think about the words you use, because they may change the minds and hearts we need to make our communities and society kinder and fairer for all.

Making the world a kinder place isn't as easy as just being smiley and kind all the time. Sometimes we have to talk and think about it, and then act on it. We have to be brave and kind enough to change minds and hearts through our words and our actions.

In his story, Connor writes about the power of language, proving kind words really do make a difference in someone's day, year, and life. I've found that in my own life, and I do my best to talk to myself—and others—using kind words because I believe, as Connor writes, that kindness ripples, as does unkindness. To ensure a more inclusive community that respects and protects the rights of people with intellectual and developmental disabilities, please visit The Arc and connect with your local chapter.

Lady Gaga

What can you do to make today—and tomorrow—a kinder place for others?

You may have heard it many times, but it's worth putting out this reminder:

Kindness is always possible,
always an option.

45

A FRONT-ROW SEAT TO KINDNESS

MAYA ENISTA SMITH

As powerful as it is to be someone who commits acts of kindness, it can also be the most extraordinary experience to witness an act of kindness done by someone simply because it was the right thing to do. This story is from Maya Enista Smith, executive director of Born This Way Foundation.

It's pouring rain in Northern California, and I'm just sitting down, getting ready to start an action-packed day of work, preparing for #KickOffForKindness, and planning an epic Year Of Kindness. After an early start, I dashed out to my local Starbucks and am back at my desk, where I—of course—already have my coffee in hand. That coffee is one of the few things that got me out of my office today.

My job is kindness, and it's incredible. I've committed to thinking about kindness beyond the fact that I'm lucky to have it as the number-one deliverable on my work plan: How is the world kinder because of your work today? I'd love to expand the answer to that question and think about what it means for me as a mom, as a community member, as a wife, as a friend.

The story most on my mind for now, though, is a lesson I learned over the past two days. I share it in the hope that it reminds you to not only think about kindness, look for kindness, and practice kindness, but also to acknowledge kindness in others.

Yesterday, on my daily coffee run to Starbucks, I ran into my good friend Heidi and her daughter.

Heidi's beautiful three-year-old is undergoing brain surgery tomorrow to remove tumors that are causing seizures in her little body. Heidi's daughter bounced around Starbucks and asked me (as she usually does) if she could have a cookie. I know what cookies can do to three-year-olds at 10:00 a.m., but this time I didn't even look at Heidi for permission. I picked her daughter up and asked her to point to the cookie she wanted, and as we waited in line to pay, I gestured to Gina (the manager) and quietly informed her of the surgery.

Mother to mother, I mouthed, Can you even imagine? *Gina and I shook our heads at each other, and she handed the little girl her cookie.*

Blinking back tears, I hugged Heidi, waved at Gina, then left Starbucks and went to work.

An hour later, I received a text from Heidi with a beautiful picture of her daughter, hugging a Starbucks bear. She wrote, "Your baristas are the best."

Gina had given her a bear to keep her company in the hospital, and with that bear, Gina gave Heidi kindness, acknowledgment, and recognition of her incredible strength and courage.

Heidi needed the kindness of someone she didn't know, someone who could do something for her little girl that a child would treasure. (Sometimes you need an outsider to cheer up your child because you are so worn out and worried.) It was a little thing, but it meant the world to me to know Heidi was given an unexpected—but much appreciated—act of kindness from a stranger ahead of a difficult, uncertain time.

I kept this story of kindness to myself . . . mostly.

Earlier today—one day later—I stood in line at the same Starbucks to order the same coffee from the same friendly faces. Gina asked me urgently if there was news and when I would know about the results of the surgery. Did they need anything else? She had just been talking to her district manager (who was seated in the store at a corner table) about the little girl and how moving it was to meet her. I promised to keep her updated and thanked her for the cup of coffee. I got in my car, preoccupied by a memo I had to write, and thought about the story that had just unfolded at this store over the past two days.

The strangers who had been kind to me, to my friend, and to each other, had done so without the expectation of anything in return. Only I had the full picture of the depth of Heidi's fear around the surgery, the joy that Gina's simple action had brought her daughter, and the genuine concern Gina had for the child of a stranger. I sat in my car, took out a business card, and wrote a note to the district manager. I went back into the store, handed her the card without a word, and ran out.

"Hi. My name is Maya. I work for Lady Gaga's foundation. I'm a huge fan of Starbucks. This is my local store and I just want to let you know that your baristas are wonderful. Gina, Kelly, + Derek are so kind, hardworking, and thoughtful. They make my day + the day of so many. Thanks!"

Now, I have a lot of work to do and writing this has taken up a chunk of my morning, but it was worth it. I had a front-row seat to kindness this week, and I wanted to tell everyone about it. Being a witness to kindness is a gift.

Two years later, Heidi and her daughter are doing really well. Nobody imagines what they can go through until they must, and then, when they do, they find the courage they need from within and, hopefully, the kindness of coffee, cookies, teddy bears, and community from without.

Please look for kindness in your world and treasure it.

♡

Hi, Maya! Thank you for all that you do to share and amplify kindness through Born This Way Foundation and in your community (most often, in a Starbucks). I love that you notice kindness when others are engaging in it and that you use our platform to share those stories. I am so glad Heidi and Gina were able to be there for each other that day to help lift the other's burden just a little bit. I hope you, and everyone reading this, keep sharing stories with our team at Born This Way Foundation, and don't forget to tag them #ChannelKindness.

Lady Gaga

46

THE
COURAGE
DIFFERENT

TO BE
AND KIND

— NICK ALBRITTON

Why would Nick Albritton, a transgender man and creative, leave rural Texas to move across the country? What motivated his efforts as a career coordinator helping young people experiencing homelessness in Seattle overcome societal barriers on the road to building a life reflective of their worth?

Nick's answers to those questions took him back to a moment in his childhood:

My father's brow was furrowed in despair as he reached for the thin wad of cash in his pocket. "This is all I got," he said to me as he thumbed past a few dollar bills and found his last $20. I cradled the loaf of bread, can of Chef Boyardee, and bottle of sugary soda as we made our way toward the door.

The twisting knot in my stomach was two parts hunger and one part shame. Shame for needing. Shame for not having enough.

I was familiar with this feeling, though. My family understood poverty. It was woven into the script I'd been born into: that corporate America was broken. That the business taxes on our family's old convenience store had run it into the ground. That the system had failed us.

My father had a good work ethic; he rose with the sun and set with it, too. He poured his blood, sweat, and tears into our family's farm. We were rich in a certain way—with hard work, swimming holes, grassy fields, and animal life. None of the green had faces on it, though, and if it did, it didn't last long.

As Nick grew into his teens, he recalled, that shame before dinner had grown with him. His self-image formed around a deepening awareness of the binaries set up by society. Rich or poor. Healthy or unhealthy. Normal or abnormal.

Rather than inhabit the shell of the identity that society imposed on him, however, Nick chose to be the person he was meant to be:

I knew at an early age that I was different. That I came from difference. Being poor was one thing; being transgender was a layer deeper.

Rural Texas didn't create much space for a kid like me, and because I had lost my mother in a tragic car accident at a young age, most people just thought I hadn't been taught how to be a proper woman. It'll take me a lifetime to heal from those wounds, but I'll continue to do that healing as the man I am today.

As adrift and alone as Nick felt, miraculous messages of kindness and encouragement arrived just in time. One of those came in the middle of senior year, when his high school band director informed him that his talent and skill were strong enough to earn him a scholarship to a large state university:

My band director sat with me as I wrote an email requesting information about scholarship auditions. As the day approached, I printed directions at the local library (this was pre–Google Maps, plus I didn't have a phone) and borrowed my grandma's car to drive two hours east to the university.

That's how I found myself, at sixteen, standing in an orchestra audition room. The flute I'd borrowed from my high school was resting in my sweaty palms.

I'd decided to play a four-page solo that I'd memorized for a state competition my freshman year. In front of an intimidating panel of professors, before striking my first note, I took one powerful in-breath. The middle section was a blur of muscle memory as I gave in to melody, allowing myself to fill the room with my love for playing music. Whatever was going to happen next, I didn't know; I only knew that nothing existed in that space except for creation. It was freedom in so many ways. I let my final note echo in the room before I exited to the waiting area.

As I sat picking at the raised red fabric of the chair, a soft voice interrupted my quiet.

"Are you here alone?" a woman said, peering at me kindly. She had short red hair and a gentle smile.

"Yes." I nodded.

More questions followed. "How do you think you did?" "Where are you from?" "How old are you?"

Her kindness put me at ease so much, we were soon laughing and carrying on like we were old friends, even family. Then she offered to buy me a meal so we could continue our conversation. We stayed in touch, and when news arrived that I'd been awarded the scholarship, she was among the first to know.

After that, she helped me fill out financial aid paperwork and drove me back and forth to community college so I could take prerequisite courses. When school officially started, I was taken into her home—where I lived with her and her family for close to a year.

Nick acknowledges that what changed his life were those moments and connections with kind and compassionate adults who gave him opportunities, who sat with him and listened, who helped in the small ways they could.

There were no quick fixes, no one-stop shop for unlearning trauma. But kindness helped, and it still does.

Nick observed that power every day when he worked at YouthCare, an organization in Seattle that works to end youth homelessness and to ensure that young people are valued for who they are and empowered to achieve their potential. YouthCare offers resources for outreach, basic services, emergency shelter, housing, counseling, education, and employment training—where Nick focused his attention. From interview skills, to resumes, to customer service, to obtaining legal identification or an internship, he helped.

He underscores that there aren't easy remedies for curing the systemic issues that result in the homelessness of teens and young adults. From his own struggles, he knows all too well that these youth have been underserved by a broken system, that too many of his clients are widely dismissed as lazy or undeserving by uncaring people who never even spoke to them.

That may be one reason why Nick refuses to give up.

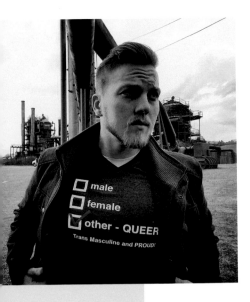

Every interaction I have with a client reminds me of how many times I myself had to try again, and still do. Each young person I meet in my work says something that takes me back to mistakes that I made in my own youth, out of pain or ignorance or a feeling of unworthiness. These youth deserve adults who give them opportunities. They deserve to be cared about and to have programming offered to them that helps them heal.

So many people in our society operate under the belief that if troubled or at-risk youth just worked harder, they could change their circumstances. But they need opportunities. They need room to make mistakes and to hear that they can come back and try again. They need teachers, counselors, internships, and job opportunities that understand they're using the tools that they have and the strategies they've developed for survival.

If we can instill hope in their lives, if we can give them relief from shame, if we can work to untangle the lies they've believed about themselves, we can help change their lives.

I know that I alone can't fix a broken system, that I alone won't be the miracle in any kid's life. But maybe I can help them send an e-mail that unlocks a positive fresh start. Maybe that e-mail can get them an audition. Maybe the woman they meet there in the waiting room will become like a mom to them and offer her spare bedroom, rent-free. And maybe that audition will lead to a scholarship offer. And they'll learn that their bravery to keep trying gets them places. That the kindness of others does make a difference. That the negative things they believe about themselves now won't always be their truth.

Ultimately, Nick Albritton works as tirelessly as he does because he is committed to kindness:

Maybe our youth will see that if they keep showing up, that we, as a society—as caring adults and committed social workers— will keep showing up, too.

♥

It takes an ample amount of courage to unapologetically be who you are. And I'm so proud of you for being unapologetically you, Nick. Not only have you worked through difficult struggles growing up, but you have retained your kindness and loving heart through it all. To stay gentle in a sometimes-cruel world also takes courage. Thank you for using that courage to show up for all the young people you worked with at YouthCare. Everyone needs someone to show up for them, and I'm comforted in knowing that you were that person for so many young people. If you'd like to follow Nick's example and show up for a young person experiencing homelessness, check out YouthCare or the Ali Forney Center.

Lady Gaga

47

THE POWER
OF INVESTING
IN OUR YOUTH

JOSH
HOLLIN

When Zoe Terry stepped out onto the stage of a TEDxYouth@Miami conference to tell her story, she was only nine years old.

She had a lot to say about how it felt to be bullied as a little girl for the brown color of her skin and her puffy hair. After suffering a stroke as a toddler, she was bullied at age five for not being very coordinated. Instead of giving in to the bullies, Zoe had the idea to encourage herself and others just like her to know how beautiful she and they really are. Her brainstorm was to create her own enterprise to get brown-skinned dolls into the hands of girls like herself and put smiles on their faces. Thus, Zoe's Dolls—of which she is the CEO and founder—was born.

Zoe's mother recalls the challenge that she had always encountered in finding dolls that resembled her daughter in any way. Most of them, she explained, were similar to white dolls in their features and appearance, only looking as if they had brown paint covering them. Zoe's passion was not only to get dolls into the hands of other girls of color but also to take a powerful stand against bullies.

Her company and her success as a young entrepreneur helped her create a platform for her message. "I wanted to let little brown girls know that their image is beautiful no matter what anyone else says," Zoe recalls.

In her TEDx Talk and subsequent media interviews, there's a statement she asks audiences to repeat. "Say 'I'm beautiful!'" Zoe directs the girls listening to her.

"I'm beautiful!" they respond in a triumphant chorus, almost like a call-and-response in church.

Having her own doll that looks like her is proof, Zoe smiles. "I am beautiful. Being different is not bad. My school helped me know that. My mom helped me know that. So that is when I got my idea to turn my bad situation into a good situation. I just wanted to make a difference."

Her policy is for every doll sold, she gives a doll to a girl in need. Between 2016 and 2020, Zoe's Dolls gave away twenty thousand dolls across the United States, Haiti, Cuba, and countries across Africa.

Over Christmases past, Zoe has partnered with celebrities like Serena Williams and sponsors who have enabled her to deliver Zoe's Dolls to girls in various South Florida neighborhoods near where she is growing up. Their reactions are priceless.

Zoe was delighted, recalling, "One girl I gave a doll to, she named her Ms. Cocoa. She had darker skin, and the doll had darker skin like her, so it really, really looked like her, and she was so excited. I remember she gave me the biggest hug, and she was just so happy that she finally got a doll in her image."

There are messages in the boxes that Zoe's Dolls come in. In the city of Miami Gardens, Florida, one recipient joyfully read her note aloud. "It says, 'I'm beautiful and I'm loved.'" A different recipient kept staring at her own doll. Finally, she explained, "I feel like it's me in a box."

When Zoe was honored with the 2017 Nickelodeon HALO Award—which stands for "helping and leading others"—Nick Cannon commended her. "You're showing girls everywhere that the sky's the limit," he said, "not only through your work with Zoe's Dolls but [by] becoming the youngest HALO honoree ever."

Zoe has even received grants to hold trainings that help motivate other "girlpreneurs" pursuing their paths as change-makers.

Zoe has powerful and kind words of advice. "Believe in yourself," she tells others of all ages, even when no one else does. "Believe in yourself and just don't give up. When you see a problem, fix it. Just fix it, and if you keep at it, you will have a business."

The advice that Zoe's mom has added to that is also important. All along, she insisted that Zoe call all the shots, and she asserts that if parents want to see their kids flourish, the kindest, most important thing they can do is just to listen, be supportive when asked, and get out of the way.

It's true that by letting kids find their own wings, they may run the risk of falling. Or they may just fly.

This story is proof that there is no age requirement to make a difference in the world. It is so important that children see themselves in the toys that they play with, and Zoe's Dolls provides that representation for so many young girls across the world. Josh's story also reminds us how beautiful we all really are; so why not start embracing your beauty today? Josh, you are beautiful. And reader, you are, too. Because baby, you were born this way! I challenge you to tell three people they're beautiful, and while you're at it, check out Zoe's Dolls to support Zoe in her mission to remind brown girls that their skin is beautiful, too.

Lady Gaga

48

FROM CHAOS TO CARING

ASHLEY LOPEZ

Anyone meeting human dynamo Ruby Guillen for the first time might suspect the truth— that she is a modern-day superhero. Few are able to guess that this same powerhouse, whose work includes saving children from violence and rescuing them from the worst imaginable child abuse, was once a foster child herself.

"I saw things, and I had experiences that didn't make me feel good," she says. "Having an understanding of that, I wanted to figure out how to make the system less scary for kids."

Not surprisingly, that led to her calling as a social worker for her community. Armed with only a badge, a clipboard, and a compassionate heart, part of her job entails driving all over Southern California, rescuing children from dangerous situations.

Ruby makes it known that even with growing public awareness of the abuse, neglect, and mistreatment of babies and children, there are far too many who desperately need to be saved. The national organization Childhelp reports that more than four children die daily from abuse in the United States. According to the American Society for the Positive Care of Children, the most vulnerable children are age four or younger, as they are at higher risk of dying.

Refusing to give up on even one child, Ruby's mission is to change those dire statistics.

And here's where her superhero reputation comes in. It turns out that when she is not physically out on the front lines protecting children, Ruby is busy creating life-saving technology that has changed the landscape of reporting on child abuse in her field.

In 2016, Ruby founded Humanistic Technologies, an enterprise focused on improving the efficiency of social workers and others in the helping fields through the use of applications and other tech tools. A primary focus of the apps aims to reduce child fatalities and help protect children from harm.

Her multiple perspectives as a former foster kid and fearless social worker, with her unique "hacktivist approach," have set her apart and made her a formidable foe of those who commit or tolerate acts of violence against children.

Ruby and her team at Humanistic Technologies have developed an app that has been pivotal in the protection of children and youth. With existing practices, when a first responder helps an abused child, the responder must file a report for their specific department. Sometimes, however, the report is not readily accessible to other departments. The app allows for these forms to be filled out online and additionally ensures that no child abuse reporting data gets lost between city departments. Keeping this data available across all city departments doubly protects children from further harm.

Ruby recognizes that no app or piece of technology can do the work that a feeling, concerned human being can. She acknowledges, "People think technology is cold." In the hands of a human being who cares, however, all that changes. She goes on. "You get a sentiment of coldness and try to create warmness out of it."

Without a doubt, kindness, compassion, and empathy are at the heart of the work of Humanistic Technologies. Take, for example, the landmark event that took place in December of 2017, when Humanistic Technologies partnered with municipalities to organize a "heartfelt hackathon" in downtown Los Angeles.

Several programmers and social workers spent days collaborating on the creation of new technology aimed not only at intervention but also at the prevention of child abuse. The Child Abuse Prevention Hackathon was the first of its kind. Unlike most hackathons that develop technology to be used in industry for investment or for profit, this event did not have cash prizes. All participants selflessly devoted their time for the greater good.

Ashley's story is proof that we can use what we learn in the face of adversity to help those in similar situations. I am grateful for compassionate people like Ruby and Ashley (a constant kindness ambassador in all that she does), who use their skills to help children. If you or someone you know is experiencing child abuse, please contact the Childhelp National Child Abuse Hotline for 24-7 help.

Lady Gaga

Ruby says proudly, "People were working together and willing to engage in dialogue and challenge each other in collaboration for the sake of children. You have to have kindness in order to maximize the value of creating technology."

Ruby's story of being a foster kid who grew up to become a superhero on behalf of all children in need of protection is a lesson to us all. We can all learn to be tough and compassionate, tech savvy and brave. There can be no greater investment than that which we make in the future of the well-being and safety of our youngest, most vulnerable citizens.

We can all make a difference with kindness in mind—just like Ruby Guillen.

ASHLEY LOPEZ

49

CREATING A COMMUNITY

THROUGH MUSIC

MALLORY
KOLODZIEJ

In Antioch, Illinois, about an hour north of Chicago, a music store that once went by the name of Musician Makers opened its doors in 2013 and was immediately embraced by the community. Chester, the owner, made sure that the atmosphere was as welcoming as a jam session in his own living room. To all who patronized the store or even stopped by, it always felt like home.

Then, in 2015, out of the blue, Chester passed away, leaving the store to his fiancée, Tricia—who soon reopened it under the name Mad Plaid Music. To help her heal from the loss, she resolved to create a community of kindness through music.

When I first met Tricia, I had meandered into her storefront on a quest to replace the strings on my guitar. What started as an unanticipated bout of friendly conversation turned into a friendship met with the same qualities she employs to run her business: fierce passion, extraordinary grace, and unconditional kindness.

We got to talking about Chester's sudden passing, and I asked what it was that made her want to keep the store open. She explained, "The students are why I keep the music store open. Our lesson program was substantial, and the thought of displacing those students would have been heartbreaking."

When Tricia first took over the store in July 2016, there were about 120 students. In just six months, the number grew to nearly 170 students. This growth spurt had a lot to do with Tricia's dedication to creating a program that enriches and empowers students musically and as individuals.

There are fourteen music and voice instructors, all warm-hearted and highly trained. The program consists of weekly private music instruction so a student can grow at their own pace. As music teachers, many of us (including me) act not only as instructors but as active listeners for our students. Or, I should add, as a teacher in this special place, I feel a responsibility to be a positive influence on my students' musical journeys, as well as a voice of some wisdom in their life's pursuits. Teaching is wonderful but, as I learned,

providing kindness and compassion through music can be euphoric.

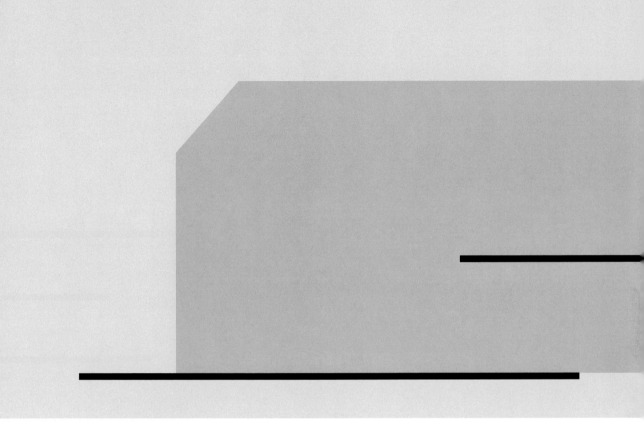

Mad Plaid Music has an inclusive atmosphere for patrons and students of all backgrounds, regardless of socioeconomic status, gender, or race. The family atmosphere means that if someone is hurting, we take care of one another. For instance, one of my vocal students' parents was unexpectedly diagnosed with cancer. When her father expressed to me that he just wanted the lives of his children to remain normal, my fellow teachers and I rallied together to raise the money needed to ensure they could continue their lessons.

Tricia recognizes that every genre and discipline of music helps us all bridge differences, and also that

"music is a good creative outlet. It speaks to everyone, no matter what language we officially speak, what country we're from, what race we are, our political affiliation, et cetera. Music is a universal language that everyone can relate to."

The store has been a safe place for folks of different ages to visit as their home away from home—almost as a kind of sanctuary. "The music store was my place to go when I was upset or not feeling well," said one vocal student who, yes, refers to Tricia as being "like family."

Lots of Mad Plaid's students get out to perform with one another in local coffee shops and schools. Tricia, Mad Plaid Music, and its teachers have instilled a passion in the students that has not only expanded their musical knowledge; it has widened the space in their hearts for giving and communicating with their peers and their communities.

Every city should have a music store like Mad Plaid Music at its center. Not every customer or student will seek a professional path as a singer or musician, but everyone who spends even a brief amount of time in the confines of the store seems to absorb the love and joy of music itself and takes a little piece of that back out with them as they go, offering it to others for the sake of simply being kind.

As an artist, I know there is a special joy, comfort, and peace found in music. I also know that music nurtures community because that's exactly where I found mine. It is through my music that I can express myself, that I can connect with fans, and that my fans can connect with me. I'm overjoyed to hear that music has brought you to a larger community, Mallory! And you're right, every city should have a music store like Mad Plaid Music. To bring the love of music to your community, check out Hungry for Music or VH1's Save the Music Foundation.

Lady Gaga

50

THE *Magic* OF KINDNESS

EMMA CARROLL

Kindness.

Why does it matter so much? More to the point, what does it *really* mean, anyway?

If you look up the word in the *Merriam-Webster Dictionary*, you'll find that kindness, a noun, is defined in the following three ways:

---

1. **the quality or state of being kind**—treating people with kindness and respect.

2. **a kind deed:** FAVOR (They did me a great kindness.)

3. **archaic:** AFFECTION

We define it a little differently at Born This Way Foundation. Kindness, we like to say, can best be defined as: **Doing something for someone else without expecting anything in return**. As individuals and as a team, we strive for kindness every day—to empower, change, and enrich lives, to bond us more closely to one another, to replace loneliness with belonging, and to help make this a kinder, braver world.

Kindness, I have seen over and over, has a power that we all too often underestimate. Kindness is a force of nature—in deeds that are small or large, whether performed by other people for us *or* by us for others. Kindness can literally be lifesaving.

And it is magical.

For most of my life—for reasons you'll soon see—I've understood the need to be shown kindness. But it wasn't until I was eighteen years old and going through a particularly painful passage that I learned how necessary it is to offer kindness to someone else—even to someone who, from all appearances and by almost every standard, might appear to be on the absolute top of the world.

Though I've struggled for years to find beauty in my brokenness, it's fair to say that I didn't exactly have the easiest start. Born three months premature, weighing only two pounds and one ounce, the odds were stacked against me. After I sustained a brain bleed at birth, upon reviewing scans of my brain, doctors predicted that if I survived, it was highly likely I would have cerebral palsy—an umbrella term for a group of disorders that impair movement, and in some cases, cognitive function as well.

The former part of their prediction ultimately came to pass. I've been in a wheelchair my entire life, am considered a quadriplegic, and much of my childhood was spent in and out of hospitals. Medical care made a huge difference—at least thirty procedures and surgeries so far—but kindness was the thing that really saved me.

Kindness saved me, as I lay crying, contorted in pain and physical illness, during the early hours of one morning after an invasive surgery to put my dysplastic hips back in my socket—for the second time. During recovery, my nurses rarely left me alone as I suffered through the agony of having had my femur broken and realigned. In a body-cast that went from the tips of my toes to just below my ribs—a glow-in-the-dark, plaster shell—I was unable to lie in my bed lower than a forty-five-degree angle.

Kindness saved me whenever my team of doctors had to break bad news, especially after we discovered I would need an incredibly risky spinal fusion surgery to correct severe neuromuscular scoliosis. Their confidence, concern, and caring helped give me the courage to go ahead with the eight-hour surgery and endure the worst pain I've ever felt. Their kindness helped me find my faith that God had put me in their capable hands and that I would make it through.

Kindness saved me in the wake of two baclofen pump overdoses that could have killed me but instead left me hospitalized, horribly sick and traumatized. Other children, themselves patients on the floor, boosted my spirits by offering me their toys and their time. Their compassion gave me a sense of normalcy when I needed it most.

And, of course, kindness saved me when, by some kind of magical stroke of good luck, I received an invitation to the Born Brave Bus, the celebrated bus that followed the Born This Way Ball throughout North America in 2013.

No one mentioned anything about the possibility that I might meet Lady Gaga. All I knew was that visits had been organized on behalf of Born This Way Foundation. Naturally, at eighteen years old, all I could think was that this was absolutely *rad*.

When I think about my life before and after that February day, it's as if I'm looking at two different versions of myself. Before that day, I saw myself as broken, unworthy, unlovable, unkind. Beyond the many challenges of my childhood, I'd been haunted by depression for years, not to mention the problems of my physical health, once again on a downward spiral. Shortly before graduating high school I hit my personal rock-bottom just as symptoms of then-undiagnosed post-traumatic stress disorder (PTSD) became overwhelming.

What if I were normal?

I found myself constantly wrestling with that question, along with the completely warped idea that I didn't do enough to better my health as a child.

Why am I here?

That question taunted me too, leaving me without concrete answers.

Night after night, I would cry myself to sleep. Like many, I found solace in the message of "Born This Way" and my faith in God—that maybe, somehow, I had something to give. "If I can't be cured," I would say in my tear-soaked prayers, "please show me a sense of purpose."

That was me before February 6, 2013—when once again kindness helped me answer those questions. A new "me" was born in the moments after a petite Lady Gaga, sporting a bright neon green wig and towering high heels, entered the bus. In my imagination, she had always loomed larger than life.

51

HOW KINDNESS / CAN HEAL / OUR CITIES /

MAYOR TOM TAIT

Former mayor Tom Tait of Anaheim, California, ran on a platform of kindness and won, serving from 2010 to 2018. Read his 2017 perspective on the transformative power of kindness and how it can make our cities stronger.

Kindness is a big, powerful word. Super powerful. Kindness means doing something for someone else with no expectation. If you do something and expect a favor in return, it is no longer kindness, it is more like a contract. Kindness is moving beyond yourself. Kindness is much more than being nice. There is a love aspect to kindness.

You can sit on your couch and be nice, respectful, considerate, empathetic, and even compassionate. But to be kind, you have to get off your couch and do something for someone else. It's an action word. It's a word that can change a family, a neighborhood, a school, a city, a nation and, ultimately, our world.

Kindness often requires courage and overcoming fear. Bravery and kindness are closely linked on a deep level. Often kindness requires bravery. It is very fitting that Born This Way Foundation stresses both.

A memory about that comes to mind.

♥

Tom, I remember your passion and persistence as you led Anaheim to become the City of Kindness, and I would be remiss if I didn't tell you how in awe of you I truly am. It's your innate belief in a better tomorrow that makes everyone who knows you want to believe in a better tomorrow, too. And that starts, as you say, by being kind. Thank you for being such a fierce advocate for kindness and for setting an example of how we can all be better human beings in our schools, homes, workplaces, and communities. We can only hope more cities follow your example. To learn how to make your city a kinder and braver place, check out City of Kindness.

Lady Gaga

The year 2004 was my last year of a decade-long stint of serving as a city councilman in Anaheim, California. During my last few months in office, I noticed banners displayed around our city that said MAKE KINDNESS CONTAGIOUS. A friend of mine contacted me and suggested I meet the man who was putting these signs up. I scheduled an appointment, and he came to my office. He turned out to be a holistic doctor from Argentina, living in Anaheim, named Dr. Edward Jaievsky.

When we met, he told me a story about his daughter, Natasha, who died in an accident while they were on a family vacation. When they returned home, he said that so many friends and neighbors told stories about little six-year-old Natasha constantly writing and talking about kindness. He found beautiful works of art and impactful words about kindness tucked away in her bedroom closet and drawers. He said Natasha's wish was for a kinder world.

He then told me something very profound.

> He told me that, in medicine, one can either treat the symptoms, or one can stimulate the body to heal from within. That's what he did as a holistic doctor. He then said, "The same applies to a city . . . One can either treat the symptoms, or one can stimulate the city to heal from within . . . and I think that has something to do with kindness."

That's when the light bulb went off in my head. Maybe it was because I had just spent the last ten years attempting to treat the city's symptoms that I knew what he said was true—that there was a better way to fix our problems.

Six years later, that statement was the reason I ran for mayor under a platform of creating a culture of kindness in order to heal our city from within. The question is, *How?*

For one thing, culture is developed by a group of people adhering to specific core values. I know from business that the value of any organization comes from its culture. The best person to develop a culture in any organization is its leader. In a company, the cultural leader is typically the CEO. So, if a CEO can develop a culture in a company, I thought, why can't a mayor develop a culture in a city? And if a mayor can develop a culture of kindness, then, I believe, everything in that city will get better.

> **Imagine a city that has a culture of being kind. It's a city where one is expected to do kind acts as a sort of civic duty. It's a city where the chance of everyone doing a kind act is just a little greater than it would have been otherwise. It's a city of kindness.**

If we can make that a reality, everything gets better. Certainly crime will drop, bullying at schools will drop, senior citizen neglect will drop, addiction to alcohol and drugs will drop, and so on and so on.

We know kindness has the power to connect people and build community.

It is also the mortar that connects the blocks that build a city's social infrastructure. A community connected by acts of kindness is safer from crime and more prepared for an inevitable disaster, either natural or manmade. Kindness is what makes a city, a school, a neighborhood, or a family more resilient. It makes us healthier, individually and collectively. In fact, I think kindness is the antidote to all the bad things going on these days. And to quote Lady Gaga when she spoke to the United States Conference of Mayors in 2016: "Kindness costs nothing . . . but it's priceless."

The citizens of Anaheim refer to our home as a City of Kindness. Not that we are always kind, but that's what we are striving to be. The important thing is that we're getting there, and we're being led by the kids.

The kindergarten through sixth graders in the Anaheim Elementary School District completed one million acts of kindness. This changed the schools. Although there were no academic studies that measured the collateral effects of this effort, we do know that each individual act of kindness has the power to transform a life. And the kids did a million of them. For example, it is hard to imagine a kid being bullied in a school that's filled with so many kind acts.

The one million acts of kindness took place as an organized effort under the City of Kindness umbrella, and it had a hugely positive effect on our city. However, I believe an even greater impact comes from the countless individual acts of kindness done quietly throughout our city every day, done when no one is watching.

Engaging in a conversation with someone who is experiencing homelessness, driving a neighbor to the hospital to get her chemotherapy treatment, simply asking someone in need the question, "How can I help?"—it is those actions that will truly make Anaheim a City of Kindness. And it is all those contagious acts of kindness that will ultimately lead to Natasha's dream of a kinder world becoming a reality.

CONTINUING ON

My daughter tells us just to be kind. "The act itself is free, and it's priceless." I couldn't agree more and it's so real in these pages.

Ever since my daughter was young, she has been kind, loving, and accepting. As she told you, despite these wonderful qualities, she experienced unkind acts that led to many struggles growing up and further fueled her passion for helping others. She envisioned a world where youth would feel accepted, heard, and better equipped to deal with life's challenges, a reality she referred to as a kinder, braver world. She made a brave decision early in her career to channel her kindness and share her own personal story with her fans around the world. At first, I didn't understand, but soon came to realize the power of storytelling. I saw that as she was healing, others were healing, and in this process, she was inspiring and empowering youth to learn how she was overcoming obstacles and challenges. As a result, they began to open up and share their own stories.

Channel Kindness grew out of this authentic and beautiful connection between my daughter and her fans. Because of her courage and the courage of youth around the world to share their stories with us, we created Born This Way Foundation and eventually Channel Kindness. From the very beginning, our goal was to inspire and empower young people to find, recognize, and share the heroic acts of kindness that fill our daily lives and shape our communities.

One of the kindest and most generous acts we can perform is to share a very personal story. It is difficult and painful, but it can also help us heal and show others that there is hope.

After reading these beautiful stories, I am so proud of the young people and all of the writers who selflessly shared stories of kindness and the many ways it impacts lives.

Each and every one of the authors in this book should be commended for their vulnerability, bravery, and kindness, and I'm so appreciative of their willingness to share a part of themselves with me and with the world. To every author, I hear you and I see your journey. And I am eternally grateful that you shared your story, as this book wouldn't be possible without it. What I have learned is that when we do share our story, we give other people permission to do the same, and slowly but surely, we learn we are never really alone in our struggles.

We are reminded as we read that kindness presents itself to us in many ways: from simply saying hello and acknowledging another person who we sensed was not having the best day; to being kind to ourselves; to standing up for those who aren't included; to engaging in our communities and providing food and shelter to those experiencing homeless; and to the most devastating of all, losing a loved one and channeling that grief into positive change. The different ways in which kindness is presented in this book reinforce what I've believed all along—

we all have the ability to do good;
we all have the ability to be brave;
and we all have the ability to be kind.

I've never been more sure about our desire to have a platform led and informed by the perspective of the youth. There is no better time than the present to have your voice heard, and there is no more important or urgent time than now to be kind to one another. A great place to find inspiration is within the pages of this book. I am so inspired and motivated by these individual stories and believe even more strongly that kindness is the key that unlocks the door to a kinder, braver world.

As soon as you put this book down, or before, take note of what inspires you, check out the organizations, nonprofits, and digital resources within these pages that are also doing good, and join us on this journey. It's a brave step, and your opportunity to Channel Kindness.

Cynthia Germanotta

RESOURCES

1 **Trust Kindness**
#BeKind21 campaign • bornthisway
.foundation/current-programs/bekind21
Random Acts of Kindness Foundation •
randomactsofkindness.org

2 **The Courage to Be Kind to Yourself**
It Gets Better Project • itgetsbetter.org
The Trevor Project • thetrevorproject.org

3 **The Gift of Being Seen and Heard**
Youth Service America • ysa.org

4 **Score A Friend**
Score A Friend • scoreafriend.org
Best Buddies • bestbuddies.org

5 **The Kindness of Offering Access**
Period • period.org/get-involved

6 **Having Cake and Sharing It, Too.**
Idealist • idealist.org/en
Volunteer Match • volunteermatch.org

7 **The Art of Kindness**
The Dreaming Zebra Foundation •
dreamingzebra.org
Feed Art • artfeeds.org

8 **Kindness in Sports**
Good Sport Club • goodsportclub.org
Playworks • playworks.org

9 **Kindness Creates Cool**
National Alliance to End Homelessness •
endhomelessness.org
National Coalition for the Homeless •
nationalhomeless.org

10 **Bicycle Journeys of Hope**
The Ability Experience •
abilityexperience.org
Youth Service America • ysa.org

11 **Kindness at The Cat House**
The Cat House on the Kings •
cathouseonthekings.com
The Humane Society • humanesociety.org
Best Friends Animal Society •
bestfriends.org

12 **The Choose Love Movement**
Jesse Lewis Choose Love Movement •
jesselewischooselove.org

13 **The Nine-Year-Old Hero**
Channel Kindness • ChannelKindness.org

14 **Learning to Heal a Broken Heart**
Stomp Out Bullying •
stompoutbullying.org
The Cybersmile Foundation •
cybersmile.org

15 **The Gift of Asking for Help**
To Write Love on Her Arms •
twloha.com
Project Semicolon •
projectsemicolon.com

16 **Memories Can Sometimes
Be the Best Medicine**
The Dougy Center • dougy.org
**The National Alliance for Grieving
Children** • childrengrieve.org

17 **Poetic Forms of Engagement**
Power Poetry • powerpoetry.org

18 **Helping Transgender Youth**
Trans Lifeline • translifeline.org
Human Rights Campaign • hrc.org
**Lambda Legal Defense and
Education Fund** • lambdalegal.org

19 **It Takes a While to Learn to Be Human**
StoryCorps • storycorps.org
The Moth • themoth.org

20 **From New York Bystander to Brave Ally**
The Accompany Project •
arabamericanny.org/accompany
Hate Has No Home Here •
hatehasnohomehere.org

21 **Only with Consent**
Rape, Abuse & Incest National Network •
rainn.org
It's On Us • itsonus.org

History of the
CHANNEL KINDNESS PROGRAM

Channel Kindness is a digital platform launched by Lady Gaga's Born This Way Foundation with the purpose of empowering young people to create a kinder and braver world. Through the power of storytelling, we hope to inspire our audience to spread kindness, encourage acceptance, and elevate the stories of good that happen in our communities every day.

Since launching in 2017, Born This Way has enlisted and trained one hundred Channel Kindness reporters to use their ears, eyes, and hearts to find, recognize, and share the everyday and heroic acts of kindness that fill our daily lives and shape our communities. By amplifying these stories on ChannelKindness.org, we hope to inspire everyone to put compassion into action in their own lives through community engagement and storytelling. Channel Kindness reporters have produced hundreds of stories of kindness, counterbalancing the negative narratives that dominate the media about young people, and instead highlight how today's young people are a wonderfully passionate, collaborative, and diverse generation.

channelkindness.org

THANK YOU

for reading this Feiwel & Friends book.
The friends who made *Channel Kindness* possible are:

Jean Feiwel, Publisher

Liz Szabla, Associate Publisher

Rich Deas, Senior Creative Director

Holly West, Senior Editor

Anna Roberto, Senior Editor

Kat Brzozowski, Senior Editor

Dawn Ryan, Senior Managing Editor

Kim Waymer, Senior Production Manager

Erin Siu, Assistant Editor

Emily Settle, Associate Editor

Rachel Diebel, Assistant Editor

Foyinsi Adegbonmire, Editorial Assistant

Mallory Grigg, Art Director

Trisha Previte, Associate Designer

A special thank you to Miriam Eichler-Rivas.

Follow us on Facebook or visit us online at mackids.com.
Our books are friends for life.

ACKNOWLEDGMENTS
from Cynthia Germanotta

My daughter and I are so grateful and full of love for the world and the stories that have been shared with us and have inspired us to spread kindness. I say this on behalf of our team at Born This Way Foundation: our Executive Director, Maya Enista Smith; Alex Aide; Shadille Estepan; Mitu Yilma; Susan Horrell; Risa Vierra; Josh Meredith; Jasmine Moniz; and Aysha Mahmood, whose efforts and amazing relationships with our Channel Kindness reporters helped shape these stories into such powerful and influential works of kindness. Thank you to Emma Carroll for naming this project Channel Kindness. What beautiful words you chose.

To each and every young person who has contributed to Born This Way Foundation's Channel Kindness Program, we love and appreciate all of you. Your voice is needed and valued in this world, and we can't wait to see who joins you in sharing more stories of kindness and bravery.

In this book, we've begun to fill all the negative space with kind things. If you want, use your own pen to write on the pages and fill all the spaces you can think of. We even made a spot for you here to share your story. I hope to read all your notes as you mark up our book. It is in these moments I know both you and I will be channeling kindness.

Lady Gaga